BIRTHSTONE STORIES

BIRTHSTONE STORIES

Discover the gemstones
of the year and their uses
in iconic jewelry

MELISE OZKARDESLER

Illustrated by
Alena Solonshchikova

VERBENA

CONTENTS

August

September

October

November

December

INTRODUCTION

———— ✳ ————

If you are someone who has even a passing interest in jewelry, you have probably given, or received, something containing a birthstone. You may love or hate your birthstone—or stones, if you are one of the lucky ones with multiple options—but have you ever stopped to consider where the idea even came from?

Birthstones have a twofold history—the ancient, and the modern. The initial concept can be traced back to a source from the 13th century BCE, the Book of Exodus, which is part of both the Torah and the Old Testament. In this ancient text, there is a description of something known as the Breastplate of Aaron, a sacred object worn over the tunic of the High Priest of the Israelites, set with 12 stones, each representing one of the 12 tribes of Israel. Modern translations of various ancient texts have tried to decipher which stones were being referenced in this breastplate, but unfortunately, the ever-changing nature of language over time has made it almost impossible to say, with certainty, what those 12 stones were.

This ancient breastplate was first associated with the concept of monthly birthstones by a historian named Josephus, who lived in Rome during the 1st century CE. He noted that there were 12 stones, 12 months of the year, and 12 zodiac signs, and assigned one stone to each month. Once again, the translations were fickle and prone to misinterpretation. Even Josephus could not be sure which stone to assign to each month, and created multiple lists. Despite this burgeoning idea of birthstones, the practice did not catch on for another thousand years, when it became customary within Christianity to associate stones with the 12 apostles, and to wear one stone per month in their honor. This practice was, of course, reserved for royalty and the very wealthy—owning 12 different gems would have been exorbitantly costly.

A TRADITION STARTS TO GROW

The practice of wearing a stone to indicate one's birth month most likely began in earnest in 16th-century Germany, although whatever list they were using to determine the stones has been lost to time. This early practice of wearing birthstones was most likely still rooted in the Christian tradition of honoring saints, with a birthstone doing double duty as a personal symbol and a religious one. It became an increasingly popular concept in Victorian-era Europe, where customs and traditions were heavily steeped in symbolism, and adornment was all the rage. By this time, colonialism—and the looting that came with it—had brought entirely new minerals to Europe from the New World, making gemstones more affordable and accessible than they had been previously. Famed jeweler Tiffany & Co. was pushing the idea of birthstone jewelry as early as the 1870s.

This history would be incomplete without mentioning an Eastern tradition regarding birthstones. There is an ancient practice in Hinduism, Jainism, and Buddhism, of assigning a birthstone based on the celestial forces that govern a person, as calculated by their birthdate. One of nine stones, known collectively in Sanskrit as *navaratna*, is determined by an astrological chart, which is drawn up at birth. These stones include ruby for the sun, pearl for the moon, red coral for Mars, emerald for Mercury, yellow sapphire for Jupiter, diamond for Venus, blue sapphire for Saturn, hessonite garnet for a celestial concept known as Rahu (the ascending lunar node), and cat's eye for its opposite, the celestial concept known as Ketu (the descending lunar node). The time and date of a person's birth determines not only which of these nine stones a person should wear, but the exact size of the stone, as well. These stones, when chosen appropriately, are said to convey great spiritual and health benefits.

It is still unclear how we ended up with the recognized, formalized list of gems that is used as a reference point for this book. Simply put, the first attempt to make a cohesive list of stones was a clever marketing ploy. In 1912, a group called the American National Retail Jewelers Association (now Jewelers of America) met in Kansas, in order to pin down a standardized list of birthstones. The intention was to amend, or add to, the generally accepted "classical" birthstones in order to ensure that every month had transparent gems that could be cut as faceted stones, or en cabochon. The idea was that these stones would look best together when crafted into "Mother's Jewelry"—pieces containing all of the birthstones of a mother's children, still a very popular gift today.

Many countries and regions of the world have their own lists of birthstones, such as Japan, with a list composed of 28 stones, including coral and jade.

AN EVER-GROWING LIST

The original list was as follows: garnet for January, amethyst for February, bloodstone and aquamarine for March, diamond for April, emerald for May, pearl and moonstone for June, ruby for July, sardonyx and peridot for August, sapphire for September, opal for October, topaz for November, and turquoise and lapis lazuli for December (curiously, the only month without a transparent stone). The list was updated again in 1952, when the main birthstone for March was switched to aquamarine and bloodstone became secondary. There was also the addition of alexandrite for June, pink tourmaline for October, citrine for November, and the replacement of December's lapis lazuli with zircon. The list changed twice more, with tanzanite added as a third gem for December in 2002, and spinel joining peridot for August in 2016. The desire to add transparent stones in 1912, and to keep up with modern trends, while also upholding tradition, has led to some months having two, or even three, birthstones.

In 1937, Britain's National Association of Goldsmiths created its own standardized list, which is similar to the American one. Notably (and generously), it includes some more readily available and less costly stones for the months that are graced with cardinal stones—rock crystal alongside diamond for April, chrysoprase alongside emerald for May, carnelian alongside ruby for July, and lapis lazuli alongside sapphire for September.

Whether you love or hate your birthstone(s), perhaps this history, and the stories behind each sparkling gem, will give you greater insight into why these particular minerals have captivated humanity for so long, in some cases for millennia.

MOHS SCALE OF HARDNESS

Throughout this book, gemstones are described as having a particular hardness on the Mohs scale. Most people are aware that diamond is an incredibly durable material, but they may not know the "hardness" of other stones. Introduced in 1812, and named for the German geologist and mineralogist Friedrich Mohs, the Mohs scale serves as a way to rank the hardness of gemstones and minerals through their ability to be scratched by harder material (and their own ability to scratch softer material). The scale is ordered from 1 to 10, with 1 being the softest mineral, talc, and 10 being the hardest, diamond. The Mohs scale is what is known as an "ordinal scale," meaning that the order of categories is important, but the exact difference between each category is not. For instance, sapphire (9) is twice as hard as topaz (8), but diamond (10) is four times as hard as sapphire. The difference in hardness between each number on the scale varies, and is not precisely known.

Birthstones on the Mohs Scale

BIRTHSTONE	MONTH	HARDNESS
Pearl	June	2.5–4.5
Turquoise	December	5–6
Opal	October	5.5–6.5
Moonstone	June	6–6.5
Tanzanite	December	6–6.5
Bloodstone	March	6.5–7
Sardonyx	August	6.5–7
Peridot	August	6.5–7
Garnet	January	6.5–7.5
Amethyst	February	7
Citrine	November	7
Tourmaline	October	7–7.5
Zircon	December	7.5
Emerald	May	7.5–8
Aquamarine	March	7.5–8
Spinel	August	7.5–8
Topaz	November	8
Alexandrite	June	8.5
Ruby	July	9
Sapphire	September	9
Diamond	April	10

JANUARY

Garnet

✳

The first birthstone of the year also happens to
have one of the longest histories, spanning more
than 5,000 years: moody, luminous, beloved garnet.
Garnet takes its name from *granatum*, an Ancient
Greek word for the deep-red pomegranate seeds that
the stone resembles, though garnet actually comes in
a wide array of colors alongside the well-known red.

Garnet

Garnet has a second, far less attractive name, carbuncle, which was used for just about any red or orange stone until the end of the 18th century, when methods for distinguishing gemstones of similar colors were first established. The term "carbuncle" is also used in the medical world, where it describes a type of abscess. Needless to say, the word has fallen out of favor when describing red gemstones. After all, who wants to have their beautiful gems associated with a pustulent boil?

ANCIENT ARTIFACTS

The earliest known garnet jewelry dates back to approximately 3100 BCE, in the form of necklaces found in Ancient Egyptian tombs. The Ancient Egyptians mined garnets in the Nile delta, and considered the stone a symbol of life and vitality. Garnets were also associated with Sekhmet, the powerful goddess of war, and the hot midday sun. They were used widely in Ancient Egyptian jewelry, often as inlays alongside other colorful gems such as carnelian, turquoise, and lapis lazuli.

Garnet in cubic form

The Ancient Greeks also placed particular importance on garnets, as their resemblance to pomegranate seeds tied them to the myth of Hades, god of the Underworld, and Persephone. After kidnapping Persephone and bringing her to his realm as his bride, Hades agreed to release her back to the world of the living, but not before ensuring that she would return to him. He offered Persephone a pomegranate, from which she ate six seeds, thus binding her to the Underworld for six months of the year. The Ancient Greeks believed that this was the reason we have seasons, with the six months Persephone spends in the Underworld causing the lush, warm, green seasons of spring and summer to turn to fall and winter. Because of this myth, garnets were often given as gifts to travelers, to ensure a safe return. Greek mythology also associates these stones with Aphrodite, goddess of love and beauty, further enhancing their desirability.

Ancient Romans continued these beliefs, favoring garnets for intaglio carvings in signet rings and pendants. During this time, garnets featured in jewelry for both men and women, with men usually wearing them in the aforementioned rings, and women also wearing them as rings but also set into earrings, bracelets, and necklaces.

Garnet features heavily in treasures found at Sutton Hoo, the site of two Anglo-Saxon cemeteries dating to the 6th and 7th centuries, located in Suffolk, England. Most famous for the presence of a large, elaborate ship burial, the site also contained dozens of intricately worked gold objects, many of them inlaid with garnet in a technique resembling cloisonné, where colored enamel is used to fill channels and enclosures made by shaping wire into various patterns. In these pieces, garnets were painstakingly cut into intricate and precise shapes, and fitted into these gold-walled channels in the place of enamel. The treasures include a stunning helmet, crafted from gold and silver, complete with eyebrows set with garnets. Among other garnet objects found at the site were pieces of a belt and buckle, a purse lid, shoulder clasps, scabbard adornments, and other sword accessories. The garnets are incredibly transparent and glass-like, revealing patterns carved into the gold settings beneath. The exceptionally fine craftsmanship, repeating geometric motifs, and use of garnets as inlay are reminiscent of pieces found in Ancient Egypt, and highlight the technical abilities and imaginative design skills practiced in the Anglo-Saxon world.

An Ancient Egyptian serpent ring, a popular design, set
with garnet cabochons. It dates from the Roman Period,
circa 30 BCE to 320 CE.

An intricate gold shoulder clasp, with garnet and glass
cloisonné inlay, from the Sutton Hoo burial mound.

TYPES OF GARNET

The survival of ancient garnet jewelry is a testament to the stone's durability. With a hardness between 6.5 and 7.5 on the Mohs scale, garnet has a long history not only as a gemstone, but also as an abrasive. Much like diamonds, the majority of mined garnets are not of gem quality. Instead, they are used for industrial purposes—as cutting agents, abrasives, and, in some cases, to aid in water filtration. When mixed with pressurized streams of water, garnet is used to cut steel. About 90 percent of the world's industrial rock garnet comes from one source, located near North Creek, New York, in the United States. Operating since 1878, it is both the largest and oldest continually used industrial garnet mine in the world. Not coincidentally, garnet is the official state stone of New York.

There are multiple types of garnet, each varying in hardness and color. The most common variety, almandine, is the deep-red gem we are most familiar with, the one that everyone thinks of when garnet is mentioned. This variety is the hardest, and the one most often used as an abrasive. Its color is caused by iron and aluminum. Almandine garnets are more likely to have inclusions and to be semitransparent.

Another variety, pyrope (stemming from a Greek word that means "firelike"), also boasts a deep-red color, but is more likely than almandine to be clear and free of inclusions. It gets its color from a mix of magnesium and iron. Bohemian garnets found in the Czech Republic and popular during the Victorian era, were pyrope garnets. Varieties also exist that are a combination of almandine and pyrope, the best known being rhodolite garnet, which gets its name from the Greek word for "rose." Rhodolite displays an enchanting, deep, purple-red color.

Tsavorite garnet in crystal form

JANUARY

Spessartine occurs in colors from orange-yellow to red-violet. A mysterious and magical mix of pyrope and spessartine—an incredibly rare blue garnet—was only recently discovered, in the 1990s. Color-change garnets are also known. These stones appear to change color depending on the frequency of light they are viewed in. The color-change phenomenon is caused by the presence of a fairly high volume of the element vanadium in the stone. Grossular garnet, colored by calcium and aluminum, occurs either as juicy, orange hessonite or the unbelievably vibrant green tsavorite, discovered in Tanzania in the 1960s and named for Kenya's Tsavo National Park. The incredibly rare uvarovite garnet produces very small, exceptionally fine, emerald-green crystals, caused by the presence of chromium, the same element responsible for the bright-green color of emeralds. Even rarer is demantoid garnet, a brilliant-green variety of andradite that flashes with a diamond-like fire. Not only is it the rarest variety of garnet, but one of the most sought-after gemstones on the planet, first discovered in Russia's Ural Mountains in the 1850s. Its name derives from the old German word for diamond, *demant*, in reference to its intense reflective qualities.

MYTHOLOGICAL AND RELIGIOUS ASSOCIATIONS

The Ancient Egyptians, Greeks, and Romans were not the only lovers of this surprisingly colorful stone. In Hindu mythology, the orange variety of grossular garnet, hessonite, is known by the name *gomedha*, and is believed to have formed from the fingernails of the powerful demon Vala, a notorious troublemaker. It is considered to be one of the nine planetary stones in Hinduism and was traditionally used as a protective talisman. In Persian mythology, garnet was believed to protect people from natural forces, such as storms and lightning. The Persians also thought the stone would lose color and turn pale to signify impending danger.

GARNET

The largest polished garnet in the world—carved in the shape of an egg—was created by master lapidary artist Manfred Wild in 2014.

Garnets also appear in the Old Testament, mentioned as one of the 12 stones in the Breastplate of Aaron (see Introduction). A giant garnet was said to light Noah's Ark during the 40 days and 40 nights that it weathered the flood. It is not surprising, then, that the stone was also used to represent the sacrifice and blood of Jesus Christ in later Christianity. In the Quran, a garnet illuminates the fourth heaven of Muslims, while the sixth heaven, where the prophet Muhammad resides, is made of garnets and rubies. Given these religious beliefs, it is understandable that garnets are still associated with protection, love, strength, and vitality in the modern world.

NOTABLE GARNETS

Like some other gems, such as sapphire and a few varieties of quartz, garnets can display the optical phenomenon known as "asterism." This is when finely scattered inclusions reflect light in such a way that it creates a pointed star pattern on the surface of the stone. Star garnets can display four- or six-pointed stars that shift across the surface when the stone is moved. This effect can only be seen when the stone is cut en cabochon—that is, smooth and domed instead of faceted. The largest known star garnet weighs a breathtaking 3,956 carats. The largest known "clear," gem-quality garnet exists in the form of a whimsical, elaborately carved egg, weighing 5,696 carats and opening up to reveal a cross set with 456 diamonds.

Prized for its incredible color as well as its large size, the largest tsavorite garnet, the Lion of Merelani, was unveiled at the Smithsonian National Museum of Natural History, in Washington, D.C., in 2023. It weighs just over 116 carats, cut down from the original rough stone of 283 carats. It represents both the largest rough tsavorite crystal ever mined, as well as the largest cut tsavorite.

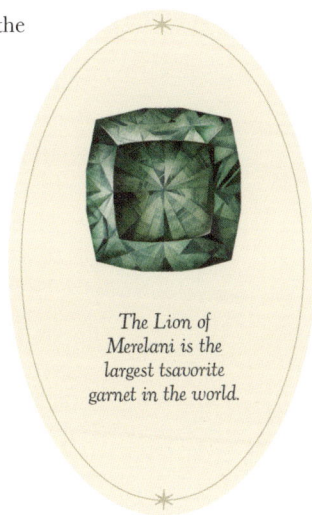

The Lion of Merelani is the largest tsavorite garnet in the world.

During the 19th century, at the height of the highly ornamented Victorian era, a variety of pyrope garnet became increasingly popular. Known as "Bohemian garnet," the deep, cherry-red stone had been discovered in the 16th century, in the form of large deposits in the hills of Bohemia in what is now the Czech Republic. Earlier examples of these luminous pyrope stones exist, but these were likely found by chance and mining did not begin in earnest until large deposits were unearthed. The exceptionally clear, cherry-red stones were recognized for their rare beauty soon after their discovery, with Venetian gem cutters traveling to Prague to teach local metalsmiths and craftspeople how to facet the stones to best showcase their glow. Demand for Bohemian garnets reached a fever pitch at the start of the 19th century, when they were sewn onto Russian dresses worn at the 1815 Vienna Congress, to celebrate the fall of Napoleon Bonaparte. Most garnet jewelry from this century is likely to be set with Bohemian garnets, usually in a rose cut, and often set in a closed-back setting. Their abundance and relative affordability kept them popular well into the start of the 20th century.

A 19th-century insect pin set with rose-cut Bohemian garnets.

Despite the enduring popularity of garnets, there are no "famous" pieces of jewelry containing the stone. The best-known piece, though likely only known to royal jewelry enthusiasts, is Princess Viggo's Garnet Kokoshnik Tiara. This style of tiara takes its name from the tall, traditional Russian headdresses that were popular from the 16th–19th centuries. Crafted for Princess Viggo of Denmark in the 1930s, by royal jeweler Aage Dragsted, this tiara is an ethereal, airy delight, with a floral garland and ribbon motif, set with garnets, diamonds, cultured pearls, and a central, natural saltwater pearl. The stunning and unusual piece is a fantastic example of the Russian influence that took hold of royal court jewelry during the late 19th and early 20th centuries. It is fitting that Princess Viggo chose to wear this unconventional gemstone in a royal tiara, because she was quite an unconventional woman herself!

Born Eleanor Margaret Green, in New York City in 1895, she was an American heiress who brought her own wealth to her marriage to Prince Viggo of Denmark. He gave up his place in the line of succession in order to marry her because she was a commoner. The Garnet Kokoshnik Tiara is just one of many beautiful and unusual tiaras that the princess owned.

It is not hard to see why garnets have captured people's imagination for so long, and why they are still so beloved today. With a variety of deep, rich hues, from sparkling cherry red to luminous, emerald green, garnet is a durable, and enduring, gemstone that continues to captivate jewelry lovers.

Princess Viggo's Garnet Kokoshnik Tiara, a rare example of a royal tiara set with garnets, surrounded by diamonds and pearls.

GARNET

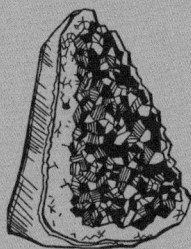

FEBRUARY

Amethyst

✳

February's birthstone might just be one of the most
popular gemstones in the world—the venerable,
grape-hued amethyst, once a member of the
cardinal stones along with diamond, ruby, sapphire,
and emerald. With a history that dates back to at
least 3000 BCE, amethyst ranges in color from the
palest of lilacs to the deepest of red-hued purples.

Amethyst

Amethyst is a variety of quartz, owing its color to the presence of iron, as well as naturally occurring irradiation. While the stone is always purple, the intensity and tone (relative lightness and darkness) of the color varies, with some of the most sought-after types of amethysts showing flashes of red and blue.

The earliest known amethyst jewelry exists in the form of three beaded gemstone-and-gold bracelets from Ancient Egypt, found in the tomb of the first dynasty king, Djer. They were found wrapped around the wrist of a linen-bound mummy of a woman, who could have been his queen or a family member. While these represent the first physical proof of amethysts featuring in jewelry, there is evidence that use of the stone goes back more than 25,000 years, with the prehistoric discovery of amethyst in France. A special, pink-hued, or mauve, variety of amethyst mined in France today is known as "rose de France."

THE BASICS

+ **Amethyst:** *A variety of quartz*

+ **Colors:** *Light purple, dark purple*

+ **Hardness:** *7*

+ **Sources:** *Brazil, Uruguay, United States, Zambia, Canada, South Korea, Russia*

23

One of the earliest known pieces of amethyst jewelry, this beaded bracelet, was found in the tomb of the Egyptian King Djer. It dates back to 3000 BCE.

NOBLE AND RELIGIOUS STATUS

Amethyst's association with royalty can be traced back to its Ancient Egyptian history during the 11th dynasty, which took place from 2050 to 1750 BCE. By this time, fine, deeply colored amethysts were being mined at a site known as Wadi el-Hudi, in southern Egypt. They were sought-after and coveted by members of the royal family and court. Inscriptions at the site of the mine suggest that it was founded during the reign of Mentuhotep IV, the last pharaoh of the 11th dynasty. It is likely that nearly all of the amethyst used in Egypt until the end of the 13th dynasty (1803–1649 BCE) came from this mine. This connection of amethyst to the royals of Ancient Egypt is a potential link to its enduring association with royalty and nobility to this day.

An amethyst geode

The name "amethyst" comes from the Ancient Greek *amethystos*, which can be translated as "not drunken," hinting at the significance the stone held in Ancient Greek culture. The Ancient Greeks thought that amethyst could prevent intoxication, going so far as to carve drinking vessels from the stone. It is a belief that tied the gem to the Greek god of wine, Bacchus. It is even noted that the color of amethyst represented the perfect dilution of wine and water—once the strong, syrupy wine of the ancient world was watered down enough to reach the pale-purple hue of amethyst, it was acceptable to drink. The mythology surrounding amethyst and its ability to promote sobriety was carried over to the Ancient Romans, who also favored the stone for intaglio carvings, often used in signet or seal rings. In a world where wine was drunk frequently, perhaps this offered a cheeky and convenient way to absolve oneself of the responsibility of drunkenness, blaming it instead on a "faulty" amethyst! The stone was worn by both men and women in Ancient Rome, where vibrantly colored gems served as an indicator of wealth and status.

Before Europeans arrived in the Americas, amethyst was unbelievably rare, reserved for royalty and the very wealthy. It also served in ecclesiastical settings, to represent the sobriety of the apostles (harkening back to the stone's Ancient Greek roots), and to discourage the clergy from becoming "drunk" with religious power. Amethyst is also one of the original stones described in the Breastplate of Aaron, in the Old Testament of the Bible (see Introduction), further cementing its symbolic importance in Christianity and the Catholic Church. Some legends state that St. Valentine wore a ring featuring an amethyst carved with an image of Cupid—a neat little tie-in to the modern, romantic holiday of Valentine's Day.

From Ancient Egypt to medieval Europe, purple was one of the most difficult colors to create naturally, making it accessible only to the richest of nobles and royals. This has always given amethyst and its rich purple hues an immediate link to royalty. The tradition of using amethyst in royal crowns endured for more than 1,000 years; the stone features in multiple pieces among the British Crown Jewels. For example, there is a very large faceted amethyst orb set into the top of the Sovereign's Sceptre, just above the astonishingly large Cullinan I Diamond.

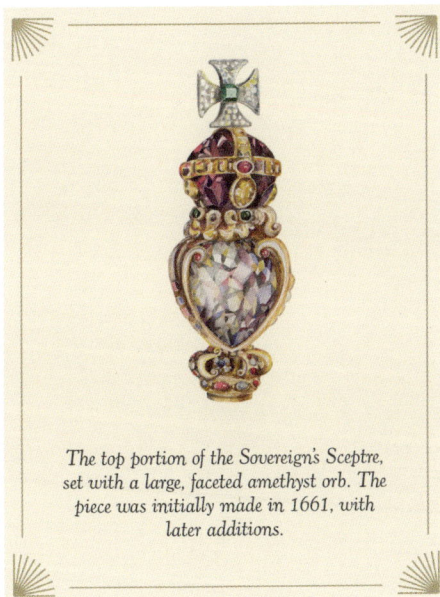

The top portion of the Sovereign's Sceptre, set with a large, faceted amethyst orb. The piece was initially made in 1661, with later additions.

AMETHYST

AMETHYST IN THE EASTERN WORLD

Amethyst's association with protective powers extends beyond the Ancient Egyptians, Greeks, and Romans, to the Eastern world. In Hindu mythology, amethyst is the stone of the crown chakra, located at the top of the head, and is associated with calmness, spirituality, and the element of air. Mentions of amethyst in Ancient Ayurvedic texts can be found as early as 1500 BCE, though it is likely that the stone was known and widely used in Southern Asia well before then. Evidence suggests that amethyst has been known and used in China since before the beginning of Chinese recorded history, around 1250 BCE. In Ancient Chinese mythology, amethyst is the stone of the dragon zodiac sign. It is also an important tool in the practice of feng shui, believed to attract wealth and help create a harmonious energy in a living space. With the arrival of Buddhism in Tibet during the 7th century CE, amethyst was associated with Buddha, and amethyst stones were used to craft prayer beads, or *mala*, giving amethyst sacred significance as a tool used in the practices of mindfulness and meditation. Today, amethyst is still associated with love, wealth, clear-headedness, and promoting a sense of calm.

AVAILABLE TO ALL

Once large deposits of amethyst were found in Brazil, in the 18th century, and taken back to Europe among other spoils of colonialism, the stone became far more available and thus affordable to more people. At this point it was no longer considered one of the cardinal stones. This must have come as a disappointment to the wealthy and royal amethyst lovers, but was a welcome change for those who could not previously have hoped to own something as precious as an amethyst. It meant that very fine, deeply colored amethysts were now within the reach of everyone, not just the richest of the rich. Historically, amethyst had come from Egypt, Sri Lanka, and Siberia, but by the 1870s, Brazil was the world's largest producer of amethyst.

NOTABLE AMETHYSTS

The largest known cut amethyst comes from Brazil, weighing just over 401 carats. This emerald-cut stone was donated to the Smithsonian National Museum of Natural History in 2012, and ranks among their largest cut gemstones. Amethyst also frequently occurs in the form of large geodes, a hollow rock lined with small, sparkling crystals. The largest amethyst geode is known as the Empress of Uruguay, hinting at its origins, and it stands an incredible 10³/₄ft (3.27m) tall.

The largest known cut amethyst, a very fine, deeply colored stone of Brazilian origin, weighing 401.52 carats.

While Brazil continues to be the world's largest supplier of amethyst, Siberia remains a source of some of the most unique and sought-after specimens. A variety known as Siberian red, originally mined in Russia, is named for its intense red flashes of color, seen when the stone is viewed from different angles, especially in sunlight. Amethyst with a similar, strong red "fire" has also been found in North America, at one notable mine in Arizona known as the Four Peaks Amethyst Mine. This variety of amethyst is exceptionally rare and commands a very high price compared to even the highest-quality amethysts, which are generally affordable.

One of the more famous examples of amethyst jewelry has to be the large, beautifully carved amethyst scarab bracelet found in the tomb of Ancient Egyptian King Tutankhamun (1341–1323 BCE). Just one of the many treasures found entombed with the young king, this striking piece consists of a band made of four strands of gold and carved gemstone beads, with a central oval-shaped setting holding a large, pale-violet-colored, carved amethyst scarab. Scarabs were an incredibly potent symbol for the Ancient Egyptians, representing rebirth, renewal, and the sun god Ra. This is only one of many scarab bracelets found in Tutankhamun's tomb, gently placed in a cartouche-shaped box to protect the king for all of eternity.

AMETHYST

Another incredible example of carved amethyst from the ancient world is a delicate, expressive miniature bust of the Ptolemaic-era Egyptian queen Arsinoë II, who ruled as both queen and pharaoh, and lived from around 316–270 BCE. This carving represents a neat piece of political propaganda, showing Arsinoë II as a chaste matron shrouded in a golden veil that perfectly frames her serene face—the societal ideal for a woman of her time. Despite this image, Arsinoë II was anything but meek. Because of her status as pharaoh, a title generally reserved for men, she was allowed to compete in the 272 BCE Olympics, and won a gold medal in two different chariot-racing events. Arsinoë II was eventually deified and worshiped as a goddess, potentially while she was still alive, though it is unclear

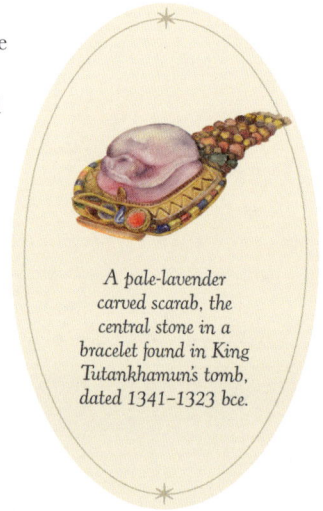

A pale-lavender carved scarab, the central stone in a bracelet found in King Tutankhamun's tomb, dated 1341–1323 bce.

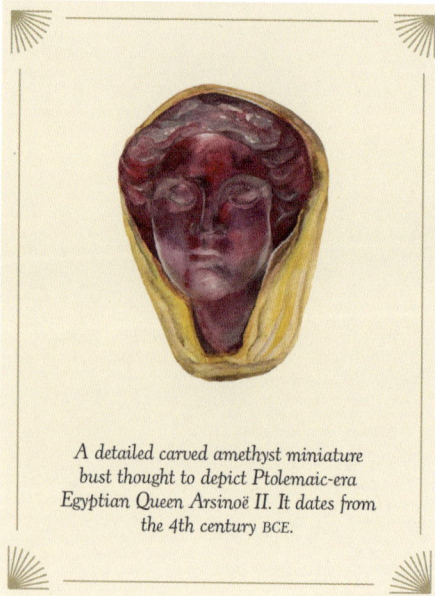

A detailed carved amethyst miniature bust thought to depict Ptolemaic-era Egyptian Queen Arsinoë II. It dates from the 4th century BCE.

if this beautiful amethyst was carved before or after her death. It is an incredible testament to a remarkable woman. The piece also highlights the skill of both the stone carver and the metalsmith who crafted the draped and pleated golden veil.

Thanks to amethyst's enduring association with wealth and royalty, it has long been a fitting choice for noble tiaras. One particularly striking example, still worn by members of the Swedish royal family, can be traced back to one of history's greatest jewelry enthusiasts, Josephine Bonaparte.

Set with incredibly fine, large, deep-purple amethysts surrounded by diamonds, this regal tiara is part of the Napoleonic Amethyst Parure, along with matching necklace, earrings, bracelet, and brooch. It is said that Josephine gave the parure as a wedding gift to her daughter-in-law, Princess Augusta of Bavaria, in 1806. She, in turn, passed it down to her own daughter, Josephine of Leuchtenberg, for her wedding to the future King Oscar I of Sweden and Norway, in 1823. It has since remained in the collection of the Swedish royal jewels, worn by countless Swedish queens FDespite amethyst's long history as a stone reserved only for the very rich and royal, it is now accessible to anyone with a taste for purple gems. Whether your preference is for pale violet, dark purple, or the striking fire-hued flash of Siberian red varieties, it is one of the most popular colored gems on the market today. Its enduring legacy is matched by its durability, making it an exceptional birthstone for everyday wear.

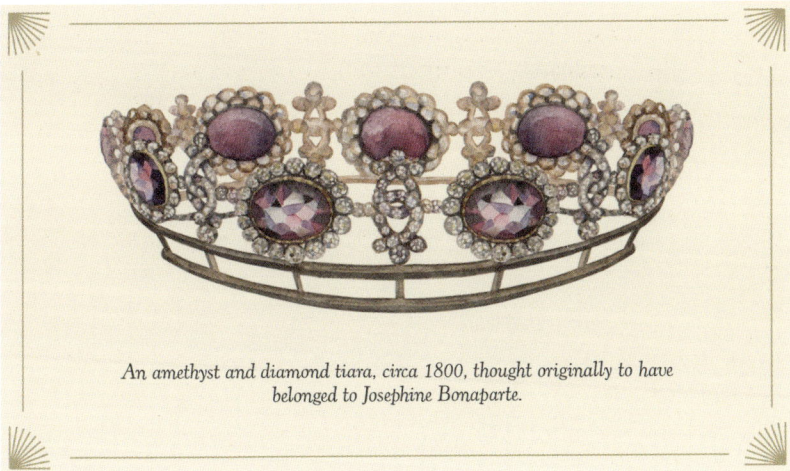

An amethyst and diamond tiara, circa 1800, thought originally to have belonged to Josephine Bonaparte.

AMETHYST

MARCH

Bloodstone - Aquamarine

✳

Bloodstone has a name that is as evocative as its history is long. It is the traditional birthstone for this month, while the beloved, sea-blue variety of beryl known as aquamarine is a modern, and more popular, choice for March. Both have an equally ancient past and share some of the same symbolism and reputation for personal protection.

Bloodstone

The earliest known bloodstone artifact is a carved seal dating back to the first dynasty of Ur, which took place from 2900 to 2700 BCE in Ancient Mesopotamia, now modern-day Iraq. Another ancient example of bloodstone, a set of round beads dating to between 2150 and 2000 BCE, was also found in the Royal Cemetery of Ur, and is believed to have originated in India.

NAMING BLOODSTONE

Though it has a history spanning more than 5,000 years, the name "bloodstone" is relatively modern compared to how long the gem has been in use. A variety of the mineral jasper, its name comes from a rather morbid medieval Christian legend that states the stone got its deep-red spots when blood dripped from Christ's wounds on the cross, staining the green jasper laying at his feet. Despite this being the most popular name for the gem, bloodstone clearly has a much longer history than the name would suggest, predating the concept of Jesus Christ by millennia.

The ancient world would have had a variety of names for it, but the one that has stuck the longest is the ancient Greek *heliotrope*, meaning "sun-turning," due to the belief that the stone would turn blood red when exposed to the rays of the setting sun. Not only popular in Ancient Mesopotamia, the stone appears in jewelry from Ancient Egypt, Greece, and Rome, as well as South Asia. In fact, the primary source for bloodstone in the ancient world would have been India.

Bloodstone

THE BASICS

+ **Bloodstone:** *A variety of chalcedony or jasper*

+ **Colors:** *Green with red spots*

+ **Hardness:** *6.5–7*

+ **Sources:** *Australia, India, Brazil, United States, Madagascar, China, Scotland, South Africa, Italy, Czech Republic, Bulgaria*

31

ANCIENT SYMBOLISM

Despite its recent name, bloodstone seems to have been associated with healing powers related to blood since at least Ancient Egyptian times. The oldest known medical text, the Ancient Egyptian *Ebers Papyrus*, dates to around 1550 BCE, and references the healing powers of bloodstone. The Ancient Egyptians also believed that the stone could grant courage, strength, and potentially even powers of invisibility, leading their warriors to carry amulets made out of bloodstone into battle. The Ancient Greeks held similar beliefs, and thought that the stone could stop a wound from bleeding, promote better circulation of the blood in the body, and increase an athlete's endurance. As with other Greek customs, the Ancient Romans adopted the same beliefs, but also thought that bloodstone could allow the wearer to control the weather, as well as protect against deception and promote justice. This last quality made it especially fitting for the stone to be carved into seals, to be set into rings or worn as pendants, and to be carried as a type of talisman known as a magic stone. These were akin to a physical form of a magic spell, often carved with images of specific deities and words, or combinations of syllables that would represent a specific intention. Today, bloodstone is still associated with courage, healing, justice, and protection.

POPULAR USES OF BLOODSTONE

An Ancient Roman bloodstone intaglio featuring a fight scene with two gladiators, and dating from the 2nd century CE.

Bloodstone has long been a favorite stone for intaglio carvings, mainly because of its dramatic coloration and durability (it has a hardness of between 6.5 and 7 on the Mohs scale). Examples have been found throughout the ancient world, including during the early days of Christianity because of its association with the blood of Christ, when it was often known by the name of "Martyr's Stone." The dramatic, spotted stones are a combination of green jasper, sometimes green chalcedony, with inclusions of hematite, a variety of iron oxide, responsible for the bright-red spots or streaks. Bloodstone composed of jasper is opaque, while bloodstone composed of chalcedony is often translucent, and this translucent variety is still occasionally referred to as heliotrope today. The most prized examples of bloodstone are a vivid, deep green color, but not so dark as to appear black, with an abundance of bright-red inclusions. Both the jasper and chalcedony varieties are equally sought-after, and stones with a glassy luster are considered most valuable.

There are many examples of ancient through Renaissance-era carved bloodstones, set into rings and pendants, but one of the most famous is an unset, carved cameo held in the collections of the Louvre Museum in Paris. Boasting an impressively detailed bust of the Holy Roman Emperor Rudolph II, it takes advantage of the natural coloration of bloodstone to create a striking contrast between the bust, which is mostly deep red, and the background, which is a vivid forest green. Rudolph II, who was a member of the Hapsburg family, ruled from 1576–1612, and it is very likely that this gem was carved for him during his lifetime.

A finely carved, high-relief bloodstone portrait cameo of Holy Roman Emperor Rudolph II.

Today, as in the ancient world, India is the largest producer of bloodstone, though other sources for gem-quality stones include the United States, Brazil, Australia, Siberia, Germany, and Scotland. Though this stone is not as popular a choice of birthstone for the month of March as aquamarine, the wealth of historical legend and symbolism, along with its durability, have ensured that it retains its spot on the list of birthstones, and still garners a devoted following of admirers and collectors.

BLOODSTONE

Aquamarine

The sea-blue variety of beryl known as aquamarine only became associated with the month of March in 1912, when the American National Retail Jewelers Association created the first standardized birthstone list. Though the stone has a long history, the name "aquamarine" is a fairly recent invention, with the first use of the word having been recorded in 1677. It comes from the Latin words *aqua*, meaning "water," and *marina*, meaning "of the sea," hinting at its longstanding association with the ocean and other bodies of water.

THE BASICS

+ **Aquamarine:** *A variety of beryl*

+ **Colors:** *Light blue, dark blue*

+ **Hardness:** *7.5–8*

+ **Sources:** *Brazil, Madagascar, Mozambique, Nigeria, Pakistan, Sri Lanka, India, China, Myanmar, United States*

34

SOURCES OF AQUAMARINE

Aquamarine

Aquamarine was first recorded by the Ancient Sumerians more than 4,000 years ago. Some references seem to have been lost in translation, and modern scholars are divided as to whether the writings refer to blue beryl (aquamarine) or colorless beryl. Given that the Ancient Greeks called both blue and colorless beryl *berrylios*, it seems likely that the Sumerians were also referring to both.

Aquamarine beads have been found with mummies in Ancient Egyptian tombs, alongside emeralds, which are a form of green beryl. It is not unreasonable to assume that, because both are varieties of beryl, aquamarine and emerald were sometimes found at the same source.

Ancient texts attribute the gemstone to Poseidon, or claim it as the treasure of mermaids, but they are notably coy when it comes to divulging the source of the stone. It is likely, however, that the ancient world was importing aquamarine from India, as well as from modern-day Pakistan, where fine, deeply colored aquamarine has recently been discovered (or potentially rediscovered). It is also possible that some of the aquamarine was coming from what the Ancient Greeks knew as the near-mythical land of Hyperborea, now modern-day Russia. Russia was the primary source of aquamarine in Europe from the 16th century until other deposits were found, and it is fair to assume that stones would have made their way to Ancient Greece and Rome via the Black Sea.

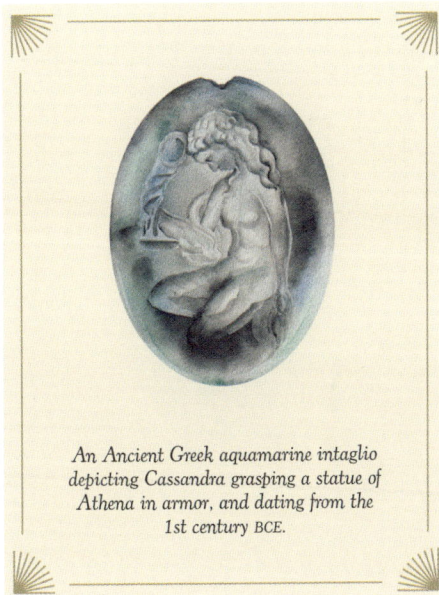

An Ancient Greek aquamarine intaglio depicting Cassandra grasping a statue of Athena in armor, and dating from the 1st century BCE.

Much like the February birthstone, amethyst, aquamarine became far more abundant with the discovery of large deposits of crystal-clear, deep-blue stones in Brazil after the arrival of Portuguese colonists in the 16th century. It is highly likely that the watery gems were "discovered" not long after, though it is reasonable to assume that the stone was known and used by pre-Columbian Indigenous cultures long before Europeans set foot on the shores of Brazil.

One of the most valuable varieties of aquamarine—known as Santa Maria, a stone of deep cerulean blue—was originally found by accident while attempting to mine for gold in Santa Maria de Itabara, Brazil. Initially discovered in the early 20th century, this variety was in such high demand that its original source is now much

AQUAMARINE

depleted. Santa Maria aquamarines owe their rich, vibrant color to the presence of higher than usual amounts of iron, the element responsible for coloring all blue beryl. The gemstone can be heat-treated to create a deeper hue, though in the world of colored gems, untreated stones with this depth of color are deemed more valuable. Today, Brazil is still the world's largest producer of aquamarine, though significant deposits are also located in Pakistan, Nigeria, Zambia, Tanzania, Zambia, Madagascar, Myanmar, Ukraine, China, the United States, and Sri Lanka. Russia no longer has enough material to mine, with their aquamarine deposits having been all but exhausted by the end of the 19th century.

ANCIENT ASSOCIATIONS

The Ancient Sumerians, Hebrews, and Egyptians associated this stone with youth, rejuvenation, and happiness. This link to rejuvenation and rebirth made it an especially fitting stone for grave goods in Ancient Egypt, where it was believed

that the deceased would be reborn in the afterlife. In Ancient Egypt and Greece, and later, Ancient Rome, aquamarine was believed to protect those going to sea, and was a favorite talisman of sailors. In fact, most cultures that used aquamarine for adornment associated it with water. In Ancient Greece, the stone quickly became associated with Poseidon, god of the sea. It was believed that an aquamarine could lose its protective powers, only to be rekindled by soaking it in seawater for an extended period of time. The Romans, so fond of folding Greek traditions into their own, similarly ascribed the stone to their god of the sea, Neptune. The Romans also believed that the stone was a powerful healing tool, and that it could aid in remedying digestive issues and edema, a buildup of fluid within tissue. In India, the stone was thought to represent love and mercy, which led to a long-standing tradition of giving aquamarines as engagement and wedding gifts. The tradition endures, and aquamarine is still given to brides on the morning after their wedding. In Hindu mythology, the stone is attributed to the ocean god, Varuna, and is tied to the throat chakra, which governs communication and self-expression.

Much like its March sibling, bloodstone, aquamarine was held in high regard by multiple ancient cultures as a stone to promote courage, as well as justice, being carried into battle by warriors and used in carved seals. As a result of these ancient beliefs, it is fitting that aquamarine is still considered to be a stone of protection, vitality, rebirth, truth, and of course, the serenity of the ocean.

AQUAMARINE

Like any other colored gemstone, the value of aquamarine is determined by its intensity of color, and tone (relative lightness or darkness of color), with pale-blue aquamarine being more common and less sought-after than deep-blue varieties. The stone is often free of visible inclusions, even at larger sizes, making it a fantastic gem for faceting and cutting.

Aquamarine is a fairly hard, if brittle, gem, which allowed the Ancient Greeks to create intricate works of art using the stone, carving it into seals, as well as miniature, three-dimensional sculptures. The Ancient Romans followed suit, and many of the existing examples of carved aquamarine date back to Ancient Rome. One of the most intriguing examples of carved aquamarine from the ancient world is a piece that bridges two distinctly different eras—that of the Roman Empire and that of Charlemagne, the first recognized emperor to rule after the fall of the Western Roman Empire. Charlemagne ruled from 768 to 814, over the Frankish kingdom that occupied lands now known as parts of France, Germany, Italy, and Spain. In the year 800, he also became emperor of the Holy Roman Empire. The aquamarine associated with him was set into a large ornamental reliquary screen, which was made of gold and various gemstones, but has since been dismantled and melted down. The only surviving piece is the crowning adornment from the top of the screen. At its center is the aquamarine, a Roman-era aquamarine intaglio, carved with the likeness of Julia Flavia, daughter of Roman Emperor Titus. This wonderfully detailed portrait was carved during the 1st century CE, and boasts an incredible, rare detail—the signature of

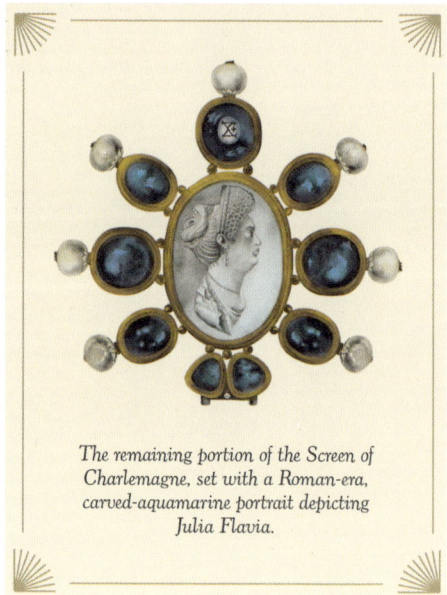

The remaining portion of the Screen of Charlemagne, set with a Roman-era, carved-aquamarine portrait depicting Julia Flavia.

the artist who carved it, the Greek engraver Euodos. It is surrounded by nine sapphires and topped with six natural pearls. The recycling of ancient gems for use by later kings and emperors is not unusual, and multiple examples of Ancient Greek and Roman cameos and intaglio show up in coronation crowns and other royal jewels.

The world's largest cut aquamarine, is also a part of one of the largest crystals ever found. It is known as the Dom Pedro Aquamarine, named for the first two emperors of Brazil. Now weighing 10,363 carats, it was cut from a behemoth of a crystal, an aquamarine originally weighing more than 225,000 carats, which was unearthed in Brazil in the 1980s. The cut stone, fashioned into a tapered obelisk with an intricate, fancy facet pattern cut into it, now resides at the Smithsonian National Museum of Natural History in Washington, D.C., mere steps from another famous blue gem, the Hope Diamond. The sparkling obelisk measures 14in (35cm) tall by 4in (10cm) wide. The unfortunate downgrade in size from more than 225,000 carats to just over 10,300 carats is a result of the original crystal fracturing into three pieces during its initial excavation. The remaining two pieces from the original gigantic crystal were cut into various pieces of jewelry, and were not left intact.

The Dom Pedro Aquamarine is the world's largest cut aquamarine, weighing 10,363 carats.

With this illustrious history, and its calming blue color, it is no surprise that aquamarine still captivates jewelry and gem lovers today. The exceptional clarity that aquamarine is known for makes it a particularly sought-after gem, and it is certainly one of the more accessible (and less fragile) members of the beryl family of stones.

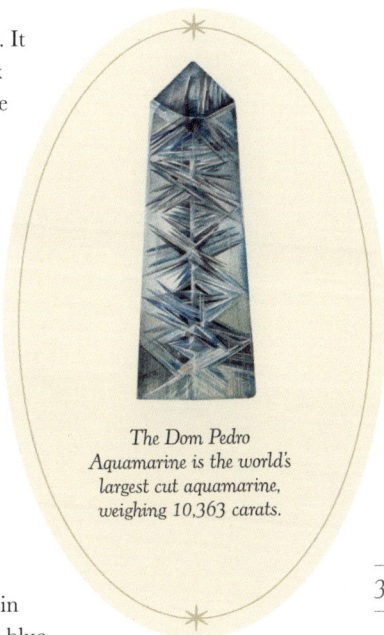

AQUAMARINE

APRIL

Diamond

✶

Perhaps the most famous, and most sought-after, of
all gems, April's venerable birthstone, the glittering
diamond, has been captivating jewelry lovers for well
over 3,000 years, if not longer. The first recorded
discovery of diamonds for use in jewelry can be
traced back to the 4th century BCE, in India, where
they were found in alluvial deposits, along riverbanks.

Diamond

An exceptionally hard and durable form of compressed carbon, diamonds are the hardest mineral on the Mohs scale of hardness, measuring 10 out of 10. In fact, they are the stone against which all other minerals are measured in order to determine their hardness. This hardness and durability means that diamonds have a long history not only as objects of adornment, but as tools, with their application as cutting and abrasive agents predating their inclusion in jewelry by a few thousand years.

There is evidence to suggest that diamond was used as a polishing agent in China as early as 2500 BCE, though it is most likely that this was in the form of diamond sand, or dust, obtained by crushing stones that would not be recognizable as gem-grade diamonds. Even today, the overwhelming majority of mined diamonds are not of the type that are set into jewelry, but are, instead, used for industrial purposes such as coating drill bits and saw blades. While they may not be as glamorous as the large, faceted, glittering stones we are familiar with, it can be argued that industrial diamonds are far more important to humanity and the development of civilization than gem diamonds ever were.

THE BASICS

+ **Diamond:** *A form of compressed carbon*

+ **Colors:** *Colorless, black, blue, green, red, pink, yellow, orange, brown, purple, gray*

+ **Hardness:** *10*

+ **Sources:** *South Africa, Canada, India, Russia, Botswana, Angola, Zimbabwe, Tanzania, Indonesia, Australia*

An octahedral diamond crystal

Despite the importance of diamonds as an industrial abrasive, they are, nonetheless, highly revered as perhaps the most refined and opulent gem in the world. Initially used in Ancient India to craft religious icons, gem-quality diamonds were, at one time, even rarer than they are today, found only in precious few Indian mines. Their rarity, coupled with their durability and clarity, made them immensely sought-after along the Silk Road, the network of trade routes that connected Asia, the Middle East, and Europe for more than 1,500 years. This meant that Indian diamonds spread as far east as China, and as far west as southern Europe, where their glitter and sparkle captivated royalty and nobility alike.

DIAMOND-CUTTING TRADITIONS

While we now associate diamonds with cut, faceted stones, the earliest examples were simply natural crystals with their flat faces polished. Because of their hardness, diamonds can only be cut and polished using other diamonds. The etymology of their name hints at this hardness, and stems from the Ancient Greek word *adamas*, meaning untameable. This word has led to some confusion when trying to untangle the early history of diamonds, however, having been used to describe other durable stones such as corundum and garnet, as well as metals such as gold. Some modern scholars assume that various Ancient Greek texts are referring to diamonds, when they were most likely referencing entirely unrelated stones. Despite this, there are examples of Greek jewelry dating back to 300 BCE, which feature diamonds alongside pink sapphires. It is also certain that diamonds were known to the Ancient Romans by the 1st century CE, because there are many examples of Roman rings set with diamond crystals.

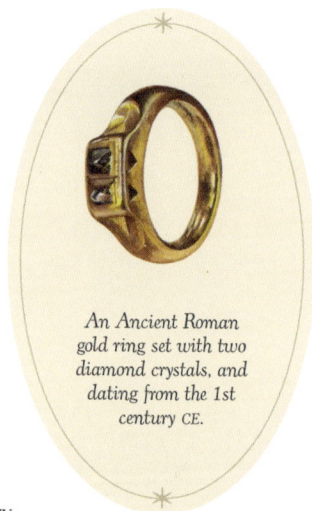

An Ancient Roman gold ring set with two diamond crystals, and dating from the 1st century CE.

While rough diamond crystals can form in a variety of shapes, some are perfect octahedrons, which look like two four-sided pyramids connected at their bases. This shape made them perfect for jewelry use, as they could be split at the center to create two identical pyramids that could then be set into jewelry without any further cutting. It was also widely believed that diamonds had protective properties that would be destroyed if a stone was worn in anything but its natural, uncut state. This meant that no one was in any particular rush to figure out the art of diamond-cutting, though it is likely that even the "rough" diamond crystals we see in ancient jewelry had some material cleaved off the crystal faces, to create a smooth and reflective appearance.

The practice of grinding up diamonds to polish other gems seems to have begun in India, around the 6th century CE. It was around this time the texts began to refer to flawed or imperfect diamonds as being inadvisable for jewelry, and only useful for grinding up and polishing other stones. It is not until the 13th century that we start to see evidence of more sophisticated diamond-cutting and polishing techniques. Indian texts from this time mention that the faces of diamond crystals cannot be polished by means of metals or other stones, but that only diamonds can polish other diamonds. This coincides with the physical evidence that we have of the earliest table-cut diamonds set into medieval Islamic jewelry, in which the points of diamond crystals would have been cleaved off to create a flat top, which was then polished to a high shine.

43

DIAMOND

The advent of diamond-cutting came to Europe about a century later, when Venice opened up trade routes to the East, and Venetian stonecutters and gem merchants learned the techniques of cleaving diamonds, as well as grinding up subpar diamonds to create polishing compound, from the Islamic merchants who were supplying them with the stones. During this time, as well as in the ancient world, it is unlikely that perfect diamond crystals were being traded outside of India. The stone was so popular there that the most desirable specimens would have been kept close to home. Islamic traders were, most likely, keeping the best examples among the diamonds they were trading. Perhaps the resulting profusion of imperfect gems is what led to the art of diamond-cutting being practiced and perfected in Europe. While the earliest cut diamonds in Europe would have been no more than imperfect crystals with their natural facets polished, the invention of continuous rotary action in tools and machines in the 15th century allowed diamond-cutting to truly flourish as an artform.

ANCIENT SYMBOLISM

Given the durability and rarity of diamonds, it is no surprise that they have been associated with strength and power in many cultures. Diamonds are one of the cardinal stones, alongside sapphire, ruby, and emerald. The Ancient Romans wore diamonds to signal their superiority over others, as they were only accessible to royalty and the incredibly wealthy. In Hindu mythology, diamonds were the weapon of choice for the god of storms and war, Indra. Because of diamond's ability to reflect and refract light, Indian beliefs surrounding the stone included its ability to "reflect" unwanted negative traits, such as disease, jealousy, and bad luck. In medieval Europe, diamonds quickly became associated with royalty, literally becoming the jewel in the crown. It is thought that the first use of diamonds in jewelry in Europe was in the crown of Queen Anastasia of Kiev in 1047, though the crown has long been lost to history, so it is impossible to verify this story. Whether or not the crown of Queen Anastasia contained diamonds, the stone quickly became a royal favorite, and has been used in crowns and royal family jewels for centuries.

DIAMOND AS A LOVE TOKEN

Though diamonds are most associated with love and commitment today, that is a relatively recent chapter in the stone's history. Starting with the discovery of diamonds in Kimberley, South Africa, in 1867, the rare and noble stone suddenly became a whole lot more accessible and abundant. The subsequent discovery of diamonds on the family farm of two Dutch immigrants, Johannes Nicolaas and Diederik Arnoldus De Beer, led to an explosion of diamonds hitting the jewelry market in the latter half of the 19th century, in what was known as the Kimberley Diamond Rush. Though the De Beer brothers quickly sold their property, the mines retained their name, and it remains one of the most recognizable names in the diamond industry today.

By the late 19th century, a cartel had formed, consolidating multiple diamond mines under the De Beers name and allowing the company to maintain an artificially inflated price for the stones by limiting the amount of diamond rough that would be sold. This development left the company with an overabundance of diamonds, leading them to hire an advertising agency that went on to create one of the most iconic ad campaigns ever. In 1947, in a stroke of genius, N.W. Ayer came up with a slogan that is still a familiar refrain today: Diamonds are forever. The slogan was used alongside a series of advertisements aimed at convincing men that their love could only be proven by spending three month's salary on a diamond engagement ring. The custom of proposing with a large, flashy diamond ring was born. Prior to this, engagement rings were made out of any number of materials and gems, but after 1947, only a diamond would do. Finally, the De Beers company had a massive new market to sell their stockpile of diamonds to.

NOTABLE DIAMONDS

While the De Beer story is a masterclass in marketing, it is not meant to devalue the beauty and elegance of diamonds. They truly are brilliant marvels of nature, and while they are not as rare as you might be led to believe, gem-quality stones of good color and clarity are not exactly a dime a dozen, either. The value of gem-quality diamonds, like that of almost all other gems, is determined by color and clarity. Diamonds are famously graded by the "four 'C's": carat weight, clarity, color, and cut. For white diamonds, the closer they are to colorless, the more valuable they are, with many diamonds showing slight yellow tones. There are, however, colored varieties of diamonds that are exceptionally rare, and highly valuable. These colored diamonds are referred to as "fancy" colored diamonds, and can be found in shades of bright-yellow, deep-brown, gray, black, green, orange, pink, purple, and blue. Red is the rarest and most expensive variety of fancy colored diamond, though they are all quite rare. It is estimated that one colored diamond is mined for every 10,000 white diamonds found.

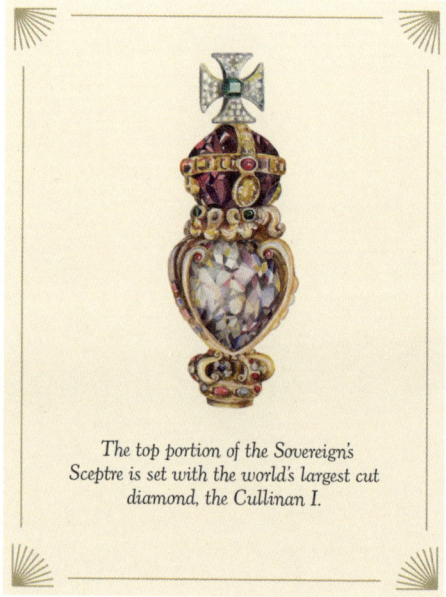

The top portion of the Sovereign's Sceptre is set with the world's largest cut diamond, the Cullinan I.

The largest cut diamond in the world is, fittingly, still in the possession of royalty, as part of the British Crown Jewels. Known as the Cullinan I Diamond, it represents a significant portion of the largest piece of gem-quality diamond rough ever found— the Cullinan Diamond—which was mined in South Africa in 1905 and weighed an astonishing 3,106 carats before being cut. The Cullinan I, also known as the Great Star of Africa, is the largest of the nine stones cut from this rough, and is a large pear-shaped stone that weighs 530 carats. It is currently set into the top of the Sovereign's Sceptre, which was first made in 1661, and was significantly redesigned to hold the massive gem.

DIAMOND

The Hope Diamond, perhaps the world's most famous diamond, is now known to be the recut French Blue.

Several other diamonds can be considered famous, but the best known is probably the Hope Diamond. A deep, alluring shade of blue, this stone has a long and remarkable history that can be traced back to 1653. Initially purchased by a gem dealer named Jean-Baptiste Tavernier, and hailing from the famed Golconda mines of India, this stone has gone through several notable adventures, including being stolen and going missing for nearly a century. Initially a 116 carat table-cut diamond, it was known as the Tavernier Blue, until it was recut for Louis XIV of France in 1668 and renamed the French Blue, by this time weighing 69 carats. It was part of the French Crown Jewels until it was stolen, along with many other royal treasures, in 1775, during the height of the French Revolution. It disappeared until 1839, when it resurfaced as a much smaller, recut stone, the Hope Diamond, now weighing 45.52 carats. Although the stone was long suspected to be a large piece of the missing French Blue, this was not officially confirmed until 2007, when a lead model of the original French Blue was found in storage at the National Museum of Natural History in Paris. The discovery of this exact replica, molded from the French Blue itself, allowed a digital model of the original stone to be made, through which it was determined that the Hope Diamond had definitely been cut from the missing stone. Unfortunately, the final cut seems to have been more of an attempt at obfuscation than beautification, and the stone has suffered a loss of sparkle and fire, though it is still breathtaking. It is now in the collection of the Smithsonian National Museum of Natural History.

Beautiful, sparkling, and seemingly indestructible, diamonds have captivated humanity since a time before we even knew how to bring out their best, and they were simply revered for their natural shape and luster. Though they have undergone multiple transformations in terms of meaning, symbolism, and perceived rarity, they remain the most coveted and popular gemstone in the world, literally and figuratively setting the standard by which all other stones are measured.

The shape of the original Tavernier Blue (top), of the French Blue (center), and of the Hope Diamond (bottom).

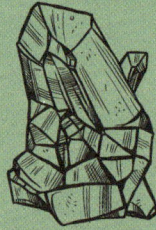

MAY

Emerald

✳

While the month of May has only one birthstone,
it is a gem so rich in both color and history, that
it has inspired countless legends, and driven
entire economies. This stone of verdant green
is so scarce that it is thought to be 20 times
rarer than diamond. In fact, emeralds are so
rare that they are one of the few gems in which
abundant inclusions are acceptable, making
stones with high clarity incredibly valuable.

Emerald

The earliest known use of emeralds can be traced back to Ancient Egypt, where they were first found around 1500 BCE. The oldest emerald mines are documented as operating since around 330 BCE. These mines, though they did not produce very much material, were in consistent use until the 18th century.

By the 14th century, deposits had also been found in India and Austria. This made the gem slightly more abundant, but it was not until the Spanish discovery and looting of much more significant emerald deposits in the Muzo emerald mines of Colombia, that emeralds became available in large enough supply to really fuel demand. Before the discovery of the mines, in 1538, the first emeralds sent back to Spain were stolen from the religious and sacred objects and statues of the Indigenous people the Spanish conquistadors encountered. Spanish mining of the Muzo deposits began in earnest in the 1560s, and did not end until the Colombian war of independence in 1810. By 1819, the mines had been requisitioned by the newly independent Colombian government, and remain under its control today. This is only a small piece of the mines' history, as it is fairly certain that the Muisca people had been extracting emeralds from these deposits as early as the 6th century. And, of course, other pre-Columbian Indigenous groups, including the Maya, Mexica, Toltecs, and Incas, had been using emeralds in their adornments and ceremonial objects long before Europeans came along.

THE BASICS

✦ **Emerald:** *A variety of beryl*

✦ **Colors:** *Medium to dark green*

✦ **Hardness:** *7.5–8*

✦ **Sources:** *Colombia, Brazil, Australia, Afghanistan, Zambia, United States, Pakistan, Russia, Madagascar, Canada*

Emerald crystals

51

Emeralds from this region of Colombia are considered to be the finest emeralds in the world, displaying a bright, alluring, saturated green color, often with a transparency and clarity that is nearly impossible to match. Colombia is still the world's largest supplier of emeralds, though deposits have recently been found in Zambia, which is the world's second-largest producer, as well as Brazil, the world's third-largest source. Smaller deposits have also been found in the United States, Canada, Pakistan, Afghanistan, Mozambique, Zimbabwe, Madagascar, Ethiopia, Australia, and Russia.

NAME, COLOR, AND CLARITY

The name "emerald" has been in use since the 14th century, and is derived from the Ancient Greek word *smaragdos*, meaning "green gem." It is a close cousin to aquamarine, as it is also a variety of the mineral beryl, and certainly the best-known stone in the family. Emerald derives its color from the presence of the elements chromium and vanadium, though some stones are colored by just one or the other. It was once thought that only beryl colored with chromium could be classed as emerald, but this idea is fast falling out of favor, and the delicate, lighter greens of

vanadium emeralds are being accepted by gemologists and gem enthusiasts as "true" emeralds. In fact, much like ruby, the lines between what are thought to be emeralds, and what are simply considered green beryl, are quite blurred, and are impacted by culture and location. Though pale-green beryl is generally not accepted as emerald, just where on the scale of color intensity a green beryl becomes an emerald can vary widely depending on who you are asking.

Unlike the other famous beryl, aquamarine, which rarely shows inclusions, emerald almost always has a multitude of visible inclusions and internal fissures. Completely clear emeralds are a very rare phenomenon in what is already a very scarce stone; they drive price up considerably. A clear emerald of a lighter color intensity will always be more valuable than a vivid emerald with many visible inclusions. The inclusions also cause emeralds to be fairly delicate, especially as far as beryl goes. Beryl itself has a decent hardness, between 7.5 and 8 on the Mohs scale, but the presence of impurities and inclusions means that emeralds are often prone to breaking. Inclusions and fissures have led to the practice of oiling stones to increase their clarity. This is a treatment in which oil, generally clear but sometimes colored, is applied to the stone. The oil settles into the internal cracks, making them less visible. While this improves the clarity and color of a stone—and is a generally accepted practice—it is also likely to hide imperfections that can lead to damage in the future, and can obfuscate the true quality of an emerald.

ANCIENT SYMBOLISM

Green is considered, by many cultures, to be the color of life, which has led to emerald's association with immortality, rebirth, and eternal youth. These ideas were especially prevalent in Ancient Egypt, and since this was one of the earliest sources of the stone, it is fitting that emerald beads and carved amulets have been found placed alongside mummies in Egyptian tombs. The infamous Ptolemaic-era Egyptian queen, Cleopatra, was so fond of the stone that she, rather selfishly, decreed that all emeralds mined in her territories were her property, and she was fond of giving them as gifts to visiting nobles and dignitaries. It is possible that Cleopatra's fascination with emeralds was influenced by Ancient Greek beliefs surrounding them, since the Ptolemaic period was marked by a melding of Greek and Egyptian ideals, with the Ptolemies being of Macedonian Greek descent. The

Greeks believed emerald symbolized love and beauty, and dedicated the stone to the goddess of love and beauty herself, Aphrodite, a goddess that Cleopatra strove to align herself with. She even went so far as to dress herself as Aphrodite for her first meeting with her Roman lover Mark Antony. The Greeks also believed that emeralds could promote fertility, and could cure certain ailments, especially of the eyes and the nervous system. Emerald amulets would be carried by those who wished to rid themselves of their ailments. The Ancient Romans, carrying over Greek beliefs into their own culture, also believed in the healing power of emeralds. It is said that emeralds would be crushed and mixed into eye ointments. The author and naturalist Pliny the Elder wrote that the color of emeralds was so soothing to the eyes, that exhausted stonecutters, after a long day of gazing upon their work, would only have to look at the stone to remedy their fatigue. He also described the verdant color of emeralds by saying, rather humorously, that "nothing greens greener."

While the Ancient Egyptians, Greeks, and Romans certainly appreciated emeralds, and had a plethora of beliefs surrounding them, there are just as many myths and legends about the stone hailing from the Americas. The Muisca people of Colombia, where some of the world's finest emeralds are found, believed that the deep-green color of emeralds represented water, fertility, and life. The Incaa considered emeralds sacred, reserving their use only for nobility and royalty, associating them with power and immortality, and believing that the stones symbolized the tears of their moon goddess, Mama Quilla. The Maya, likewise, associated emeralds with vitality, prosperity, and eternal life, as well as love, and considered them to have strong healing powers. The Mexica people called emeralds *Quetzalitzli*, because of the color's resemblance to the resplendent green plumage of the quetzal bird, and considered the stones a gift from Quetzalcoatl, the feathered serpent god of life and wind. Each of these cultures used emeralds in their sacred and religious rites, as well as wearing them for personal adornment. It may seem surprising that pre-Columbian people shared so many of the same beliefs surrounding emeralds with the Ancient Egyptians, Greeks, and Romans, but it is not so shocking when you consider that the color green is the color of plants, trees, and waters, all of the life-giving and sustaining elements that people relied on for their continued health and well-being. Today, emeralds are still an enduring symbol of renewal, vitality, love, protection, and prosperity, drawing on the gem's longstanding history as a stone associated with life and spirit.

NOTABLE EMERALDS

Given the scarcity of emeralds, as well as the rarity of gem-quality stones with good clarity, it may be surprising to know that some of the world's largest emerald crystals weigh well over 1,000 carats. The two largest examples of gem-quality emerald crystals both hail from Zambia. The biggest of these, known as the Chipembele (meaning "rhinoceros" in the Bemba language), weighs an incredible 7,525 carats, and displays a deep, lush color reminiscent of evergreen forests. The second largest crystal, the Inkalamu (the Bemba word for "lion"), is just a touch smaller than the Chipembele, at 5,655 carats. Hailing from the same Kagem mine as its larger sibling, it displays the same striking shade of green and exceptional clarity. Another massive emerald crystal from the Kagem mine, known as the Insofu ("elephant"), weighed more than 6,000 carats when it was first unearthed, but it will not remain intact. It now belongs to the venerable jewelry house, Chopard, who plan to cut the giant crystal into finished stones, to be used in their jewelry.

Another notable emerald—at one time one of the world's largest crystals—has been cut into a strangely shaped vessel, known as the Emerald Unguentarium. Initially commissioned by the Hapsburg emperor, Ferdinand III, in 1641, at the height of the emerald craze in Europe, it was carved out of an enormous Colombian Muzo emerald weighing more than 3,000 carats, almost certainly the largest known emerald crystal at the time. Its irregular shape is a testament to the artist's desire to waste as little of the original crystal as possible, and its lid and feet are fashioned from the

The Emerald Unguentarium, a vessel carved from a single Colombian emerald, dating from 1641. It is one of the largest cut emeralds in the world and weighs 2,860 carats.

material hollowed out to create the vessel. While the original weight of the crystal is unknown, the weight of the finished piece is an impressive 2,860 carats. This unusual receptacle is now in the Imperial Treasury Vienna.

Given emerald's longstanding association with royalty, it should come as no surprise that the stone has been used extensively in royal jewels. One of the most elegant examples is an elaborate diamond and emerald tiara made for the British Queen Victoria, and given to her as a gift by her husband, Prince Albert, in 1845. This striking circlet was initially part of a parure, consisting of the tiara, a pair of earrings, a necklace, and a brooch, which the queen can be seen wearing in more than one portrait. It seems she was rather fond of this extravagant emerald tiara, composed of rows of cushion-cut diamonds and step-cut emeralds, topped with a diamond scroll motif surrounding kite-shaped emeralds. The scrolls are

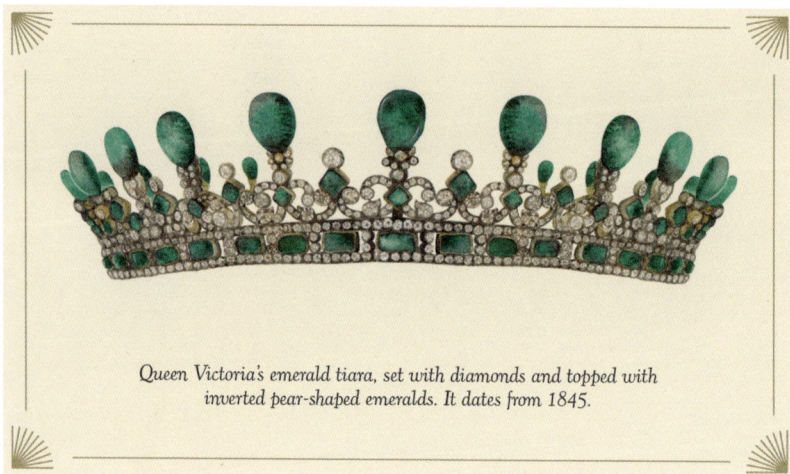

Queen Victoria's emerald tiara, set with diamonds and topped with inverted pear-shaped emeralds. It dates from 1845.

MAY

surmounted by 19 inverted pear-shaped emeralds, with a total weight of 104.5 carats. The whereabouts of this tiara were rather murky during the latter half of the 20th century, leading some to believe that it had been dismantled. Fortunately, that was not the case. The tiara eventually made its way, via multiple inheritances, to the 3rd Duke of Fife, a great-grandson of King Edward VII, who graciously loaned it to Kensington Palace for permanent display. It can be seen there now, along with the rest of the sparkling emerald parure.

Given its history as a stone embodying the forces of life, nature, and vitality, emerald's enduring popularity in the world of gems and jewelry is no surprise. Once the fabled treasure of Egyptian queens and Mexica rulers, it remains one of the most popular stones in the world, despite its rarity and relatively fragile nature.

EMERALD

JUNE

Pearl - Moonstone - Alexandrite

✳

Halfway through the year, we come to June, a month
that leaves us with the peculiar conundrum of
having three birthstones. It is also the only month
to feature a birthstone made of organic material,
as opposed to a mineral—the illustrious, and
lustrous, pearl. When grouped with the magical,
color-shifting alexandrite and the ethereal, serene
moonstone, we get our group of birthstones for June.

Pearl

Pearl is the original birthstone for this month, a stone with a truly ancient history spanning thousands of years. The earliest known example of pearl jewelry dates back to at least 520 BCE, when a Persian princess was buried with a triple-strand pearl necklace, a piece that does not look out of place alongside modern pearls. Though this is the earliest known example, it is fairly certain that pearl hunting, and the use of pearls as adornment, predate this Persian princess by millennia. For example, there is a written record of Chinese royalty receiving gifts of pearls in 2300 BCE.

THE BASICS

+ **Pearl**: A hard, lustrous, organic gem formed within the shell of an oyster

+ **Colors**: White, pink, green, blue, purple, yellow, orange, black, brown

+ **Hardness**: 2.5–4.5

+ **Sources**: China, Japan, Indonesia, India, Philippines, Australia, French Polynesia, Vietnam, Thailand, Myanmar

Pearls show up in the mythologies of every culture that has encountered them, and they were often associated with the moon. In ancient China, pearls were placed in the mouths of the deceased, to ensure a smooth passage to the afterlife, and a better life when reborn. In the Vedic texts of ancient India, pearls are thought to be the daughters of the moon, and the Hindu god Krishna is said to have encountered the first pearl, and given it to his daughter on her wedding day. The Ancient Greeks believed that pearls were tears of joy, shed by the goddess of love, Aphrodite—like the pearls, she was born of the sea. It comes as no surprise, then, that pearls still symbolize love, purity, and wisdom today.

In Ancient Rome, Julius Caesar was such a fan of pearls that he could accurately weigh them by holding them in the palm of his hand, one of his favorite party tricks. He was so enamored with pearls that he created all sorts of restrictions around their purchase, decreeing that unwed women were not allowed to own them. Pearls were so beloved that this resulted in an immediate increase in weddings! Caesar is also said to have given a sensational black pearl to his favorite mistress, Servilia. He reportedly paid a sum of six million sesterces, (roughly $2.3 billion today), making it one of the most valuable gems of all time. The fate of that particular pearl is unknown.

THE CREATION OF PEARLS

Wild pearls are made in the shells of mollusks. They are created as part of a defense mechanism when a small piece of foreign matter finds its way into the creature's mantle, a protective lining of tissue similar to skin. The mollusk, usually an oyster or mussel, will create a protective sac around this foreign matter and coat it in successive layers of nacre, the iridescent, lustrous material responsible for the shine of both pearls and mother of pearl. As a result, every wild pearl is composed of hundreds or thousands of layers of nacre alternating with a natural glue-like substance called conchiolin, tightly wrapped around the original irritant, often just a grain of sand. Nacre is not entirely opaque, and it is the buildup of many layers of translucent, iridescent nacre that gives pearls their warm glow and glossy luster. Nacre is quite a bit softer than most gemstones, and pearls require a certain amount of care to avoid scratching or damaging their surface. Naturally occurring pearls are extremely rare and highly valuable. However, inventive, clever humans have perfected the process of agitating a mollusk enough to make it produce a "cultured" pearl, and just about anyone can get their hands on a decently priced strand of pearls nowadays.

Humans have been trying to figure out how to force mollusks to create pearls since, at the very least, the 5th century BCE. Enterprising pearl merchants in Ancient China discovered that they could insert carved objects made out of shell, clay, or ceramic (usually in the shape of Buddha) into the shell of a mollusk, creating what is now known as a mabe, or blister, pearl. These differ from natural pearls in a few ways, the most notable being that they have a flat back, due to being grown within the shell and not the mantle tissue. Humans continued to try to glean the secrets of the perfect pearl over the next 2,000 years, with some interesting experiments, stops, and starts, until the late 19th century, when the mystery of

culturing pearls—by introducing a small piece of foriegn matter to the mantle—
was finally figured out by the Japanese entrepreneur Kokichi Mikimoto. Using this
method, it is possible to grow larger pearls if left in the shell longer, although the size
of a pearl is ultimately limited by the type of mollusk producing it.

In our modern world, most, if not all, pearls on the market are cultured, and
spontaneously occurring, or wild, pearls are rare and hard to come by. Of course,
they have always been rare and hard to come by. Before we had access to perfect,
on-demand natural pearls, they were jewels reserved for royalty and the richest of
nobles. Pearls had to be harvested by divers, in an age before we had things such as
diving suits and oxygen tanks. Given the spontaneous nature of a naturally occurring
pearl, it was very much a hunt. There was no guaranteeing where, or if, a pearl
would turn up. Because of the risky and difficult nature of the work, it was not
uncommon to force enslaved people to do the job. There are legends about enslaved
pearl divers finding a perfect pearl, and being able to trade it for their freedom.
The violent and dangerous history of pearls is a dark counterpoint to the properties
historically associated with them—purity, nobility, chastity, and honor.

NOTABLE PEARLS

Some of the most notable pearls are not, in fact, the perfectly round specimens that
are so coveted, but are a bit more interesting to behold. One of the most famous
is La Peregrina, which is Spanish for "the pilgrim woman," a most apt name. La
Peregrina has spent time in the jewelry boxes of many incredible women since it
was found off the coast of Panama in 1513. A substantial, 56-carat, pear-shaped
gem, it was initially gifted to King Philip II of Spain, who elevated it to the status
of royal jewel. It quickly became a favorite of many Spanish queens, showing up
in portraits and paintings of Elisabeth of Austria (one-time queen of France) and
Mariana and Margaret of Austria (both queens of Spain). It eventually ended up
in the hands of Joseph Bonaparte, older brother of famed Napoleon and one-time
king of Spain. Bonaparte sold it to the Duke of Abercorn as a gift for his wife. She
wore it often, and once even lost the pearl in the sofa cushions at Windsor Castle.
The same family owned it until 1969, when it was sold at auction to Richard Burton,
who was snatching up yet another famed jewel as a gift for his wife, jewelry collector
extraordinaire, Elizabeth Taylor.

PEARL

She nearly lost the pearl, herself. After realizing it was missing from around her neck, and frantically retracing her steps in her Las Vegas suite, she found it in the mouth of her puppy, fortunately unscathed.

Another shape of pearl that was once very highly prized is known as "baroque." These are bulbous, bubbly, organically shaped pearls that defy the perfect, smooth conventions of a round pearl. During the Renaissance, these pearls were often artfully formed into intricate pendants, with artisans and goldsmiths finding inspiration in the irregular shapes and turning pearls into the bodies of dragons and gryphons, sirens and tritons. There are baroque pearl sheep, swans, horses, and sea serpents. Just like cloud-watching, the creative eye can find a dozen different possibilities in each baroque pearl.

While pearls can come in sizes as small as one millimeter, the largest known specimen weighs nearly 600 carats. It is called the Pearl of Asia, measures 3in (7.5cm) tall, and is believed to have been found in the Persian Gulf sometime in the 16th century. The pearl is creamy white with silvery overtones, kidney shaped, and currently held in a charming, slightly strange, gold setting that resembles fruit dangling from a vine, made to fit around the pearl in the early 20th century.

The large, historically significant La Peregrina pearl,
Dating from 1513, it was beloved by Spanish queens and
Elizabeth Taylor alike.

The "Pearl of Asia," the world's largest known pearl,
weighing 600 carats.

Moonstone

In 1912, when the American National Retail Jewelers Association met to standardize the master list of birthstones, they decided to give June's classic pearl a companion—moonstone. Meant to provide a transparent alternative to the pearl, one that could be cut and faceted like other birthstones, moonstone was the perfect choice for the restrained brilliance of the early Art Deco era. Note that, when we are talking about moonstone in the context of birthstones, this does not include rainbow moonstone, which is actually a type of labradorite. This is not entirely surprising, as moonstone is a variety of feldspar, just like labradorite. Consider them siblings. The type of moonstone envisioned when the list was created in 1912 displays an effect known as adularescence, which looks like a transparent veil of white or blue moonlight shimmering in, and across, the stone. Highly prized specimens of moonstone are perfectly clear, with a distinct adularescence. While still beautiful, opaque moonstones are more common, and less valuable. Moonstone also occurs in a variety of colors, including shades of pink, orange, blue, green, and brown.

Historically, the finest, blue-sheened moonstones were unearthed in Myanmar, though they are found in many places around the world today. The most sought-after gems are mined in Sri Lanka, Myanmar, Tanzania, and India, while other varieties occur in Brazil, Mexico, Armenia, the United States, and Australia. That sought-after, mystical, ethereal sheen is caused by light bouncing off alternating layers of the minerals orthoclase and albite within the stone. The thickness of these albite crystals also affects the color of the sheen, with fine crystals resulting in a blue sheen, and thicker albite crystals resulting in white.

THE BASICS

+ **Moonstone:** *A variety of feldspar*

+ **Colors:** *Colorless, black, pink, green, brown, yellow, gray, purple*

+ **Hardness:** *6*

+ **Sources:** *Myanmar, India, Sri Lanka, United States, Mexico, Australia, Brazil, Madagascar, Tanzania, Australia, Poland, Armenia, Switzerland, Norway*

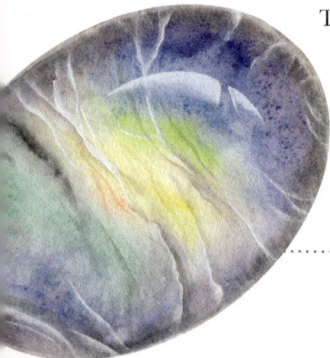

MOONSTONE MYTHOLOGY

Like its June sibling, pearl, moonstone is an ethereal, delicate, lustrous stone with ties to lunar mythology. Both the Ancient Greeks and Romans associated the stone with their lunar deities, with the Greeks believing that they were the solidified tears of the moon goddess, Selene. In fact, their name for the stone was *aphroselene*, a combination of Aphrodite, goddess of beauty, and Selene. In Hindu mythology, the stone is made from solid moonbeams (a belief shared by the Romans), and is considered especially sacred. Another name for moonstone is hecatolite, after Hecate, the Greek goddess of the Underworld, witchcraft, and, yes, the moon (a role she shared with Selene). In medieval Europe, moonstone was worn as a protective stone, especially to help guide travelers at night. Placing a moonstone in your mouth during a full moon was thought to grant psychic powers and incite premonitions. Because of these long-standing beliefs, moonstone is still considered to be a stone that promotes good fortune, emotional healing, and is thought to enhance spiritual and psychic abilities, being associated with the third-eye chakra in Hinduism and Buddhism.

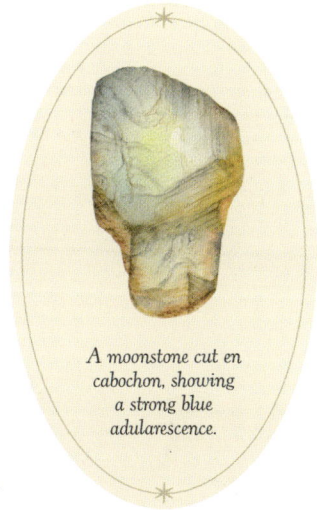

A moonstone cut en cabochon, showing a strong blue adularescence.

POPULARITY OF MOONSTONE

Though the stone has seemingly never waned in popularity, it has experienced a few waves of trendiness over the last few centuries. Queen Victoria was incredibly fond of the stone, often wearing an entwined serpent brooch set with four large moonstones. Since Queen Victoria was the fashion It-girl of her day, this all but ensured that moonstone would remain popular during her reign. It was used prominently in jewelry throughout the remainder of the 19th century, and continued to fascinate well into the 20th. In the early decades of the new century, prestigious jewelry houses such as Fabergé, Lalique, and Tiffany made pieces in the Art Nouveau and Art Deco styles, incorporating the cool, airy, barely there stone. Right around this time is when we see the stone being added to the first official birthstone list, an ancient, but perfectly modern stone for the 20th-century woman.

MOONSTONE

Moonstone is not an exceedingly rare stone, but it is very unusual to find clear, gem-quality specimens with strong adularescence weighing more than 100 carats. The largest known moonstone, while not perfectly transparent but leaning toward a milky, nearly opalescent translucence, is the size of a chicken egg, and is reputed to weigh more than 400 carats. It was found in 1918, by a group of Japanese climbers ascending Mount Kilimanjaro, in Tanzania.

Despite having a history spanning more than 3,000 years, there are no existing examples of moonstone jewelry from ancient times. This is likely due to the stone's softness, which makes it a poor candidate for surviving the centuries. There are some fantastic examples of carved moonstone seals from the 16th and 17th centuries, and they are probably not dissimilar to engraved moonstone gems worn by the Ancient Greeks and Romans. In fact, the Cheapside Hoard, a collection of jewelry dating back to the 16th and 17th centuries, contains two pieces of carved moonstone—a very charming little frog ring, and a more elaborate, rectangular engraved gem showing an annunciation scene.

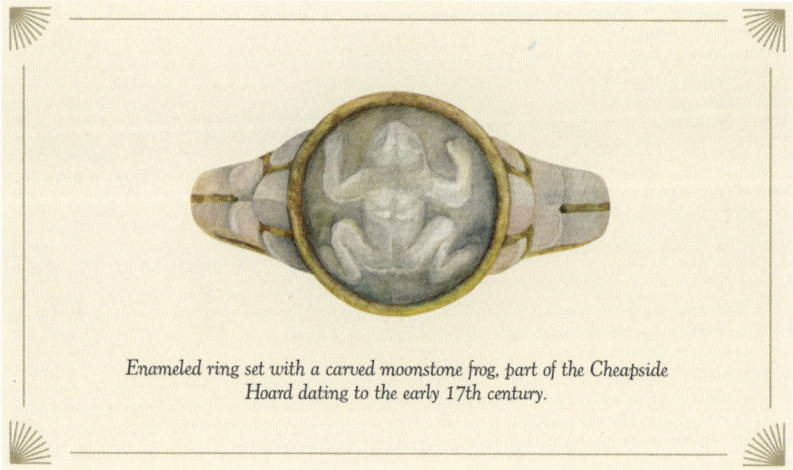

Enameled ring set with a carved moonstone frog, part of the Cheapside Hoard dating to the early 17th century.

JUNE

Alexandrite

The next of our three stones for this month is alexandrite, a fairly "new" gemstone as far as these things go. Discovered in the 1830s in the Ural Mountains of Russia, and named after Tsar Alexander II, it is a rather mysterious stone with a very unique property—it changes color, generally from a shade of blue or green to a shade of purple or red, when exposed to different wavelengths of light. (The stone was apparently named as birthday gift to Alexander, who at the time was not yet the tsar.)

THE BASICS

+ **Alexandrite:** *A variety of chrysoberyl*

+ **Colors:** *Changing from blue or green to purple or red, depending on light*

+ **Hardness:** *8.5*

+ **Sources:** *Russia, Brazil, India, Sri Lanka, Zimbabwe, Madagascar, Mexico, Australia, Myanmar*

Because these stones were initially found in emerald mines, and often appear green or teal under natural light, they were thought to be emeralds, but only until their color-shifting properties were discovered. Alexandrite is a variety of the stone chrysoberyl, and gets its color-changing properties from the presence of chromium ions, which alter the way the crystalline structure absorbs certain wavelengths of light. Our eyes are most sensitive to green, and least sensitive to red, meaning that alexandrite will appear green in daylight, where the full spectrum of light is present, and red in incandescent or artificial light, which emits less blue and green light. Because it displayed the official colors of Imperial Russia's military, and was already tied to the monarchy through its name, alexandrite quickly gained status as the official gemstone of Imperial Russia.

ALEXANDRITE

BECOMING A BIRTHSTONE

Alexandrite was the third June birthstone added to the official list, making an appearance in 1952, when the Jewelry Council of America expanded the official birthstone list for the first time since 1912. If you are aware of the incredible rarity and high price of natural alexandrite, you might think this is a foolish choice for a list of stones that should be accessible to everyone, for Mother's Day gifts and birthday presents. Why would a group of jewelry professionals add such a rare and valuable stone to the list? The Jewelry Council of America may have been betting on the growing popularity of laboratory-created alexandrite, which had been commercially available since the 1920s. That bet seems to have paid off, because a more effective and efficient method for growing alexandrite crystals was discovered in the 1960s. Gold cocktail rings holding massive, sparkling, perfectly transparent specimens of lab-grown alexandrite dominated the jewelry world during the mid-20th century, beloved by all, whether or not they had a birthday in June. These lab-grown stones often exhibit a far more extreme color shift than natural stones, usually from bright purple in artificial light to bright green in daylight.

THE VALUE OF ALEXANDRITE

Naturally occurring alexandrite can range in color from dark purple, pink, red, orange, and peach in artificial light, to varying shades of teal, blue and everything from lime to forest green in daylight. Because it is a relative newcomer to the jewelry scene, there are not any enticing historical examples of jewelry set with the stone. The rarity of these gems, coupled with the relatively small size of most alexandrite specimens, leads to some eye-watering prices, easily putting diamonds to shame. In 2014, Christie's auction house sold an unmounted, 21.41-carat Russian alexandrite for $1.4 million. A year later, Sotheby's auction house sold a 26-carat Ceylon (Sri Lankan) alexandrite for $754,000. When it comes to determining the largest known specimen of alexandrite, things get a bit murky. The majority of these stones are held in private collections, with no photos available, making it very hard to verify any claims. The largest uncut alexandrite is the Sauer Alexandrite, a crystal weighing more than 122,000 carats. It was discovered in Brazil, in 1967. The largest cut alexandrite is a trickier subject—officially, it's a 65.7-carat stone that shifts from bright, froggy green to a cognac brown, mined in Sri Lanka and held in the collections of the Smithsonian National Museum of Natural History. According to Guinness World Records, it is a 141.92-carat stone that belongs to an anonymous owner in Japan, no photographic evidence provided. There is yet another claim to the title—the 112-carat Naleem Alexandrite. Photos of this stone are available, but claims about its size have not been verified, and it is also in the private collection of an anonymous owner. This confusion about which stone takes the throne as queen of alexandrites befits the aura of mystery and magic surrounding this unusual, one-of-a-kind gem.

Though there are not any ancient or long-standing beliefs about alexandrite, its rarity and seemingly magical color-shifting properties have given it a reputation for bringing prosperity and good fortune, and promoting balance in all aspects of life.

ALEXANDRITE

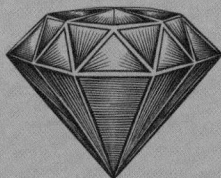

JULY

Ruby

✳

There are few colored gemstones that are as
highly prized throughout history as rubies. These
intensely red, sometimes hot-pink gems have
captivated people since at least 2500 BCE, when
rubies were first discovered in the Mogok region
of Myanmar, formerly known as Burma. Burmese
rubies, as they are known, have continued to
set the standard of quality for 4,000 years.

Ruby

There are records of rubies moving along Silk Road trade routes as early as 200 BCE, a time when the gems were already prized in most Eurasian cultures. The earliest known example of cut rubies is found in an unusual place—set into the eyes and navel of a small statuette of a goddess, (likely the hybrid goddess Ishtar-Aphrodite) carved out of translucent alabaster and wearing

THE BASICS

✦ **Ruby:** *A variety of corundum*

✦ **Colors:** *Reddish-pink to red*

✦ **Hardness:** *9*

✦ **Sources:** *Myanmar, India, Thailand, Mozambique, Afghanistan, Pakistan, Madagascar, Sri Lanka, Tanzania, Vietnam*

a crescent moon crown. This lovely little artifact dates to somewhere between 250 BCE and 250 CE, and was found in a Greco-Babylonian tomb in Hillah, near Babylon, in modern-day Iraq.

RUBY OR PINK SAPPHIRE?

A variety of corundum, the same type of mineral as sapphire, ruby differs in one regard—the presence of chromium, the element responsible for its rich red color. Rubies are one of the traditional "cardinal" gems, alongside emeralds, diamonds, and sapphires, and are incredibly durable, with a hardness of 9 on the Mohs hardness scale. The only mineral harder than ruby (and sapphire) is diamond, making it an incredibly durable choice for jewelry.

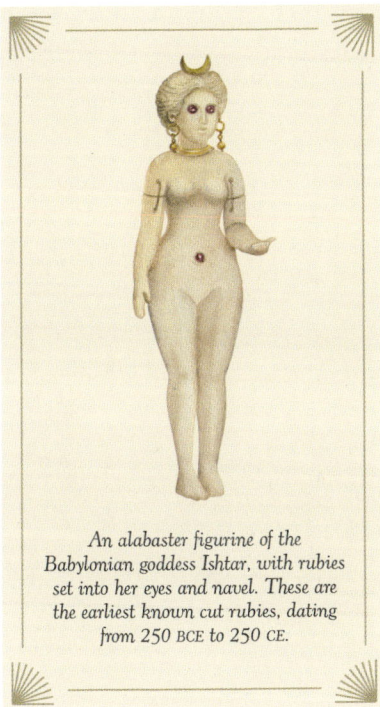

An alabaster figurine of the Babylonian goddess Ishtar, with rubies set into her eyes and navel. These are the earliest known cut rubies, dating from 250 BCE to 250 CE.

Arguments often arise as to where the line can be drawn between pink sapphire and ruby, and, historically, they have often been one and the same. It is only in recent times, and mostly in the United States, that the distinction has been made between pink and red corundum, with a minimum color saturation needed for stones to be considered rubies. Unless the stone is a true red, the difference between ruby and pink sapphire can be entirely subjective. Before the 20th century, there was no concept of "pink sapphire," just pink and red rubies. Before the 18th century, things were even muddier, with many other red or pink stones being mistaken for rubies over the course of a few thousand years. The most famous imposter is red spinel, also known as balas ruby, a stone you will get to know a little better in the next chapter, as it is one of August's birthstones. Garnet and pink tourmaline have also done double duty as ruby impersonators.

ANCIENT MYTHOLOGY

The mythology surrounding rubies is greatly influenced by their vibrant, warm color, often being associated with fire, or the sun. The Ancient Greeks believed that the stone exuded its own heat, and could get warm enough to melt wax. Ancient Romans believed that rubies could cure health conditions related to the heart and blood, due to the stone's color. In Ancient Hindu mythology, ruby is the most important of the gemstones, called *ratnaraj*, or king of the stones. It was believed that offering a fine ruby to Krishna was a sure way to guarantee reincarnation as an emperor. Rubies were also thought to help keep the wearer safe in multiple cultures, and apocryphal legends tell of Burmese soldiers inserting rubies under their flesh in an effort to achieve invincibility. Chinese noblemen adorned their shields with rubies for their protective powers. Rubies were also buried under the foundations of buildings in ancient China, to ensure good fortune. In fact, in our modern world, rubies are still associated with vitality and protection, and are linked to the heart chakra by practitioners of Hinduism and Buddhism.

THE VALUE OF RUBY

As with all other colored gemstones, the intensity and tone (relative lightness or darkness) of color is one of the determining factors of a ruby's value. The finest, and most sought-after, color of ruby is, rather morbidly, known as pigeon-blood red. It is described as a vivid, blue-toned red, with a high intensity and medium tone. A quality pigeon-blood ruby will also be very transparent,

with minimal inclusions. Transparent, gem-quality rubies of large sizes are exceptionally rare. The largest gem-quality ruby ever found, the Star of Fura, weighs 55.22 carats. Compare that to the largest diamond ever found, the Cullinan Diamond, which weighed 3,106 carats before being cut. The rarity of larger, gem-quality ruby rough is one of the reasons why it is such an expensive stone, with a fine ruby potentially costing 50 times more than a diamond of the same size. It is no surprise, then, that ruby is one of the first gemstones to have inspired man-made imitations. Examples of imitation rubies can be traced back to Ancient Rome, likely made of colored glass. In the 17th century, faux rubies were created by coloring silver foil red, and placing it under cut rock crystal. This demand for affordable rubies even drove scientific advancement, with the first synthetic rubies grown as early as 1837. A reliable process for creating synthetic rubies on a commercial scale was discovered in 1903, and lab-created rubies (as well as sapphires, which uses the same process with different trace minerals) flooded the jewelry market not long after. Synthetic rubies were not just important in the world of jewelry trends, either—lab-grown ruby was an essential component in the creation of the world's first optical laser, in 1961. Lab grown rubies and sapphires are also an important component in watchmaking.

The DeLong Star Ruby, the largest gem-quality star ruby in the world, weighing 100 carats.

ASTERISM

Star rubies deserve a special mention. These rare examples of an already rare stone, exhibit a phenomenon known as asterism. Stemming from the Ancient Greek word for star, asterism is a star-shaped reflection of light caused by the presence of an inclusion known as "silk" —minute, uniformly shaped impurities that scatter light just so. Star rubies can have four- or six-pointed stars, and the finest examples will be brightly colored, showing a centered, distinct, symmetrical star that shifts across the surface of the stone when moved. Asterism can occur in other stones as well, with star sapphires being especially popular, as well as star topaz and star garnet, but none are as valuable or sought-after as star rubies. The largest star ruby, and arguably the most famous, is the DeLong Star Ruby, a juicy 100-carat gem found in Burma (modern-day Myanmar) in the 1930s.

RUBY

HISTORICAL RUBIES

Because of the historically lax attitude toward which shade of red—let alone, which stone—actually constitutes a ruby, there are not that many straightforward, historical examples of ruby jewelry prior to the medieval era in Europe. Around the 15th century, there seems to have been a vogue for rather dainty gold rings set with single rubies, often with a flat table-cut stone, or domed en cabochon. During the Renaissance, we see rubies vying for space with emeralds and pearls on elaborate, often enameled pendants and pins. All very pretty, but if we want to go back a little bit further in history, we should take a look at Asian cultures. There are splendid examples of ruby jewelry dating back to 8th-century Central Java, in Indonesia, used to great effect in conjunction with substantial, high-carat gold settings in rings, pendants, and ear ornaments. During the same time period, rubies were in great demand in China, adorning everything from earrings to hair combs to elaborate burial headdresses.

NOTABLE RUBIES

Some of the most famous rubies can be considered quite small, as far as gemstones are concerned. There is the Cartier Sunrise Ruby, which weighs 25.59 carats and sold for an eye-watering $30.3 million in 2015. It set the record for most expensive ruby ever sold, as well as highest price per carat ($1.2 million per carat). It is a flawless, true-blood red stone from Myanmar. Another well-known ruby is the "perfect" ruby that once belonged to Elizabeth Taylor, a woman who owned quite a few illustrious jewels. Given to her as a Christmas gift by then-husband Richard Burton, the 8.24-carat, cherry-red stone was set into a diamond halo ring by renowned jewelers Van Cleef & Arpels, and dropped into her stocking for Christmas Day. She nearly overlooked it during the excitement of Christmas morning. Burton had promised Taylor that he would, one day, find her "the most perfect ruby in the world," and, though their multiple marriages did not last, the ring continued to be one of Taylor's favorite pieces of jewelry. It is now, hopefully, someone else's favorite ring, having been sold at auction, in 2011, for the incredible sum of $4.2 million.

Those with an interest in royal jewels may consider this a famous ruby, or rather, grouping of rubies—one that is still in use in crowning all queen consorts of the British

A "perfect" ruby, once owned by Elizabeth Taylor.

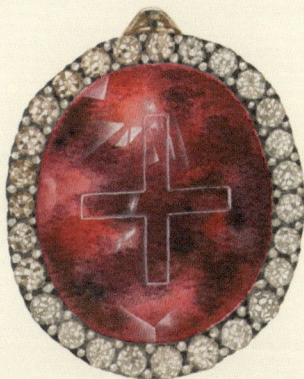

The 17th-century Stuart Coronation Ring, holding a large table-cut ruby with the cross of St. George carved into it.

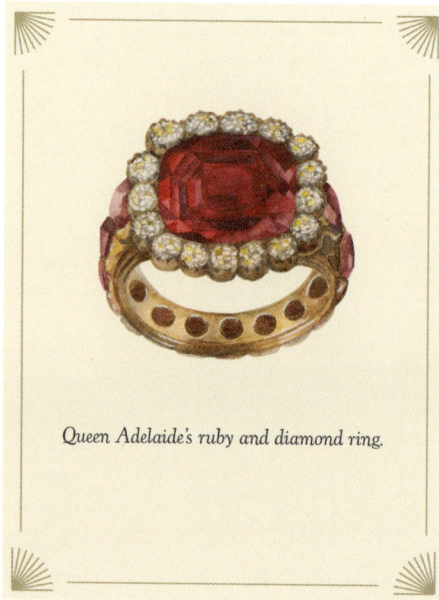

Queen Adelaide's ruby and diamond ring.

monarchy: Queen Adelaide's ring. It is also known as the Queen Consort's Ring. Crafted in 1831 for Queen Adelaide, wife of King William IV and aunt to Queen Victoria, the ring is set with a large, striking octagonal ruby that straddles the line between deep red and hot pink. It is surrounded by a halo of diamonds, with a band of 14 graduated rubies of various cuts, perfectly matched in color.

Another intriguing ruby can be found among the British Crown Jewels, the Stuart Coronation Ring. Thought to be made in the 17th century, if not earlier, it is a striking ring with a rather large, thin, central ruby, carved with the cross of St. George, and backed with foil. The foil was put in place to help light bounce back out of the closed setting, so that the deep raspberry color of the stone could be appreciated. It was used for the coronation of King James II of England, who also reigned as James VII of Scotland. An account from King James's coronation in 1685 refers to the stone as a "large Table Ruby Violet," likely because of the color's fuchsia leanings. It is hypothesized that the ruby is one half of a medieval-era bead, cut and polished to remove evidence of the drill hole. This would explain the apparent thinness of the stone, and the rather unusual cut, not one often found in rubies of this era. It also explains the need for a foil backing, a treatment that, while ancient itself, was not usually applied to rubies. The cross was most likely carved in the 17th century, probably just before the ring was crafted.

JULY

RED SPINEL

What of the most famous royal rubies, such as the Black Prince's Ruby in the Imperial State Crown of the United Kingdom, or the Timur Ruby, a massive, inscribed blood-red cabochon set into an impressive necklace, also part of the Royal Collection of the British royal family? And how about the golf-ball-sized ruby set into the top of the Imperial Crown of Russia, commissioned by none other than Catherine the Great? Or, a famous ruby in the collection of the French Crown Jewels, a fabulous, carved slumbering dragon that once adorned the same pendant as the "missing" French Blue diamond, and another in the Russian Crown Jewels, a peculiar, but adorable piece shaped like a bunch of grapes, known as Caesar's Ruby? Unfortunately, none of these examples are actually rubies! The majority of them are red spinel, once called balas rubies and thought to be a variety of ruby themselves, well into the 17th century. Caesar's Ruby is a rubellite tourmaline, a name that makes clear just how much this variety of tourmaline resembles rubies. There seems to be no shortage of historical "rubies" that are actually red spinel, with many of the examples being much larger than any known ruby. If you would like to know more about spinel, you are in luck—they are one of August's birthstones, and are further discussed in the special chapter about gemstone imposters.

It is fairly easy to see why this stone has captivated imaginations for thousands of years. It seems to be lit from within, glowing with the fire of the sun. The color comes thrillingly, disconcertingly close to the color of our own blood. It is rare, with the best stones being so scarce and remarkable that they fetch a much higher price than diamonds of comparable quality. The advent of synthesized, lab-grown rubies has contributed to the advance of science and technology, helping to create better lasers, communication devices, and, of course, watches.

RUBY

AUGUST

Sardonyx - Peridot - Spinel

✳

Coming in hot on the heels of June's three-stone
bounty, August is yet another month boasting three
birthstones: easily carved, striped sardonyx, vibrant-
green peridot, and relative newcomer, spinel. Beloved
by many ancient cultures, and popular until the 19th
century, sardonyx may not be as widely recognized
as it once was, but it is still an incredibly sought-after
stone, especially favored by cameo enthusiasts.

Sardonyx

Sardonyx is exactly what the name describes—alternating layers of sard and onyx, to create a gemstone with contrasting stripes. Sard is orange-red to brownish, while onyx is black or white, and the resulting combination creates a rather dramatically striped stone that has been in use for at least 4,000 years.

Sardonyx is a variety of the mineral chalcedony, itself a form of quartz. Chalcedony represents a large family of minerals that include many semiprecious stones, such as jasper, agate, bloodstone, and carnelian. It has a hardness between 6.5 and 7 on the Mohs scale, making it simultaneously durable enough for daily wear, and soft enough to carve. Sardonyx has a beautiful glassy, or waxy, luster, which, paired with the translucent to transparent quality of the stone, gives it a shining satin-like sheen when polished.

THE BASICS

+ **Sardonyx:** *A variety of chalcedony*

+ **Colors:** *Banded stripes of red, orange, white, black, brown, colorless*

+ **Hardness:** *6.5–7*

+ **Sources:** *India, Brazil, Germany, United States, Madagascar, Uruguay, Czech Republic, Russia, Slovakia*

A red, white, and orange sardonyx cut en cabochon.

A HISTORY OF CARVING

The earliest known sardonyx artifacts can be dated back to Ancient Egypt, during the second dynasty, which took place between 2890 and 2670 BCE. One hints at the prevalence and importance of this stone in the ancient world: a royal scepter made of tubular sardonyx beads held together with gold fittings, that was found in the tomb of King Khasekhemwy, who reigned from 2676 to 2649 BCE. Sardonyx was highly prized for the ease with which it could be carved, and a competent stone carver could take advantage of the alternating layers of color in a single stone to create wonderfully detailed images. Likely because of its ability to be carved and shaped into all manner of talismans, Ancient Egyptians believed that sardonyx had the power to ward off evil spirits and carved it into various shapes, including that of the ever-present scarab beetle. This gave the stone a second layer of symbolism, taking on the attributes of whatever it was cut to resemble. Sardonyx was also revered in India, where Hindu legends associated the stone with strength, stability, and protection. Some myths state that sardonyx was created by the god Vishnu, to protect the earth from negative energies.

The art of carving sardonyx into intricate scenes and portraits really flourished during the Hellenistic period in Ancient Greece, the time between 323 and 31 BCE. During this period, skilled artisans began carving incredibly detailed scenes from fables and religious myths into the colored layers of the stone, as well as busts and portraits of gods and members of royalty. The Ancient Romans, always eager to adopt Greek culture, took this practice and elevated it even further, creating some of the most astonishing works of art.

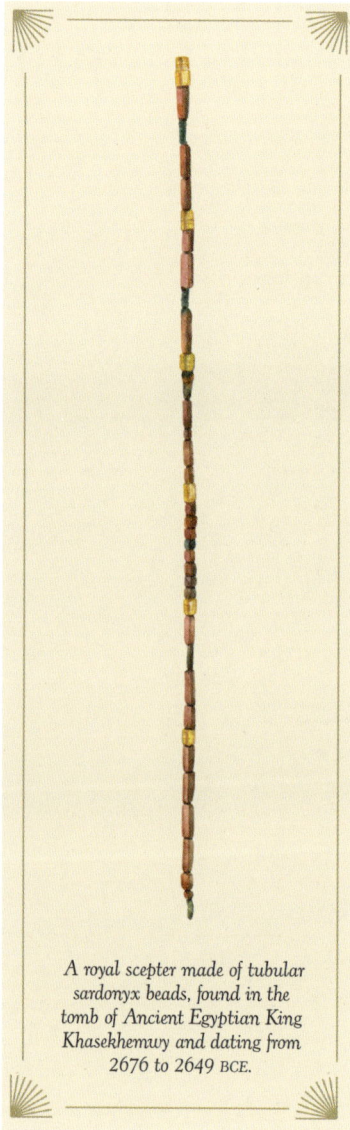

A royal scepter made of tubular sardonyx beads, found in the tomb of Ancient Egyptian King Khasekhemwy and dating from 2676 to 2649 BCE.

In both Ancient Greece and Rome, sardonyx carvings of figures such as the gods Hercules and Zeus (Heracles and Jupiter, for the Romans) were worn by soldiers in battle, with the belief that the protective powers of the stone would absorb the qualities of the figures they were carved with, and impart them to the wearer. Though sardonyx was an abundant, inexpensive stone, such skilled carvings elevated it immediately to one of wealth and luxury, as only the rich could afford to commission and buy such beautifully carved works of art.

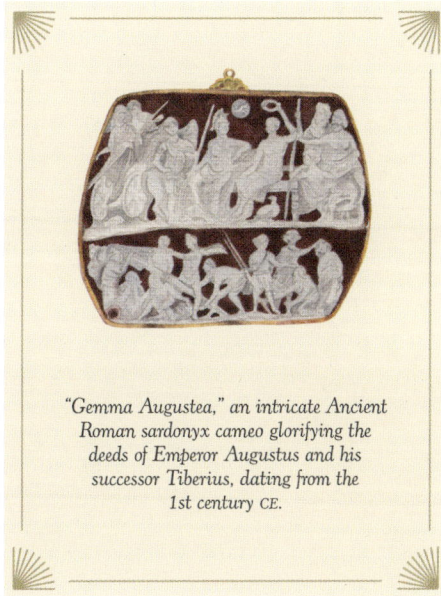

"Gemma Augustea," an intricate Ancient Roman sardonyx cameo glorifying the deeds of Emperor Augustus and his successor Tiberius, dating from the 1st century CE.

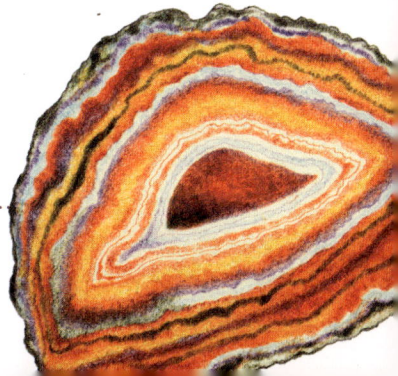

SARDONYX

SARDONYX SEALS

One of the traits that made sardonyx particularly useful for carved seals and signet rings is that, unlike more porous stones, hot wax does not stick to sardonyx. Some of the oldest known carved sardonyx seals can be traced back to the ancient Minoans, and would have already been in use around 1400 BCE. More than one carved seal has been found bearing Bactrian writing (Ancient Iranian, with a script derived from the Greek alphabet) and Hindu gods. One of the more elaborate examples is one that portrays Vishnu blessing the Hun king Mihirakula, who ruled over northwestern India in the 6th century. Mihirakula is remembered as a vile and violent king— certainly not a man worthy of any god's blessing—and this delicately carved seal, now in the collections of the British Museum, likely represents a bit of propaganda, the king's attempt to align himself with divinity to further rationalize his brutal deeds. The ancient Sasanians, the last pre-Islamic empire of Iran and successors of the Parthians, were also very fond of sardonyx seals. There are some lovely, intricate seals carved with images of Sasanian queens and nobles, some in strikingly dramatic colors, used to great effect in the layered elaborate carvings.

82

A carved Bactrian sardonyx seal with an image of Vishnu facing a kneeling worshipper. Found in Pakistan, it dates from the 4th century CE.

A carved Sasanian sardonyx seal with an image of Queen Yazdan-Friy Shapur, and dating from the 4th century CE.

ENDURING APPEAL

The practice of carving sardonyx into beautiful intaglios and cameos remained popular into the medieval and Renaissance periods in Europe, continuing to be used as a stone of protection, as well as taking on the properties of whatever symbols and images were carved into it. In fact, until very recently, sardonyx was the stone of choice for carving all manner of cameos, usually utilizing a white or black layer of onyx to carve figures against a brown or red background of sard, though some more intricate examples can show three or four layers of color.

New carvings were continuing to be created, and ancient carvings were also being re-used in contemporary settings. Napoleon Bonaparte famously commissioned a crown he called the "Crown of Charlemagne," alleging that it had belonged to the king of the same name (it did not), using a pastiche of ancient carved intaglios and cameos, many of them made out of sardonyx. Napoleon had a rather extensive habit of utilizing ancient carved stones, and newly crafted copies, in an attempt to create a link between himself and the emperors of classical Rome, just one of many forms of propaganda he employed to legitimize his various campaigns.

Sardonyx has largely fallen out of favor in the use of modern jewelry, but there are many collectors who still seek out ancient and antique examples of finely carved intaglios and cameos. It may no longer be commonly regarded as having protective powers—or the shifting, chameleon-like ability to take on the properties of the images carved into it—but it is still highly prized by those who have an eye for fine craftsmanship and classical symbolism.

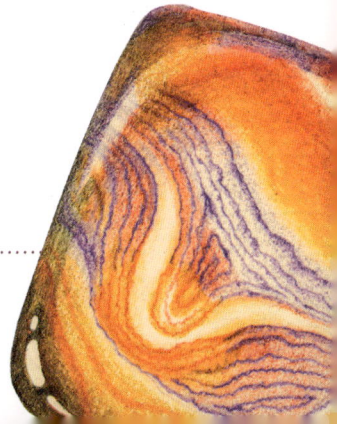

SARDONYX

Peridot

Of all of the naturally occurring gems that have made their way into jewelry and adornments across time, there are few that are as vibrant and intense as peridot. Added to the official birthstone list as one of August's stones, when it was formalized in 1912, peridot is a stone that seems to be a bit polarizing— either you love it, or you do not. Peridot is not a stone that invites calm, moderated affection, but rather, zealous devotion, among those who do love it.

THE BASICS

+ **Peridot:** *A variety of olivine*

+ **Colors:** *Olive green*

+ **Hardness:** 6.5–7

+ **Sources:** *Pakistan, Myanmar, China, Egypt, United States, Vietnam, Italy, Finland, Australia, Kenya, Tanzania, South Africa, Sri Lanka, Saudi Arabia*

ANCIENT ORIGINS

Ranging in color from a dramatic, dark, brownish, olive green to what can only be described as neon lime green, peridot has been prized since at least 1500 BCE, which is when it was first referenced in ancient papyri. It was mined by the Ancient Egyptians on a small volcanic island in the Red Sea—known as Zabargad Island today, but called Topazios at the time. With a name like Topazios, it is not unrealistic to expect the island to offer up topaz, rather than peridot. This misnomer can be attributed to the fact that peridot was initially known as topaz. The name was changed for unknown reasons in the 18th century. It is unclear whether peridot was simply mistaken for topaz, or if it was given a new name so that the old one could be used for the golden-brown stone that we now call topaz, and which captivated Europe during the 18th century. Given the vibrant color of peridot, it is fitting that the Ancient Egyptians called it "the gem of the sun," and kept its source a secret. The location of the ancient peridot mines was not rediscovered until the early 20th century, though any meaningful deposits of the stone had long since been depleted.

Peridot crystal

An Ancient Egyptian carved peridot depicting a goddess,
likely the oldest known carved peridot in the world,
dating from 1550–1295 BCE.

One of the oldest examples of peridot from the ancient world is a small, carved, dark-green stone dating to the 18th dynasty of Ancient Egypt, which took place from 1550 to 1292 BCE. It is carved with an image of a goddess, likely Hathor, the goddess of motherhood, fertility, love, and the sky, holding an ankh, the symbol of life. That this "gem of the sun" should have been carved into a talisman representing life seems most appropriate. It may have been intended to ward off bad dreams and negative thoughts. Legends state that peridot was mined at night, given the heat of the sun on the small island of Topazios, and it was said that the gem shone even brighter in the moonlight, giving it the nickname of "evening emerald." It is also thought that some of Cleopatra's famed and beloved emeralds were, in fact, peridot.

Since Egypt maintained tight control over their peridot-mining operations, the country was also the main source of the stone for the rest of the ancient world. The Greeks cherished peridot, associating it with the god Zeus, and believing that it brought prosperity and good fortune. It is possible that the name "peridot" comes from the Greek word *peridona*, meaning "giving plenty," though it has also been posited that the name comes from the Arabic word *faridat*, which means "gem."

PERIDOT

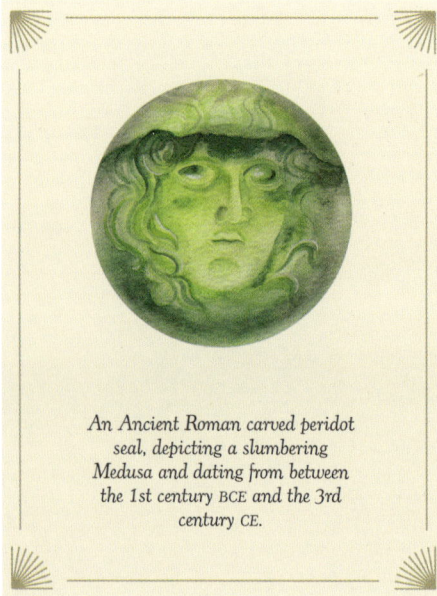

An Ancient Roman carved peridot seal, depicting a slumbering Medusa and dating from between the 1st century BCE and the 3rd century CE.

The Ancient Romans, often following the lead of the Greeks, also dedicated the stone to their version of Zeus, Jupiter, and ascribed similar properties of abundance and prosperity to it. Both Greeks and Romans also adopted the Egyptian belief that peridot could ward off negative energies and evil spirits, carving it into talismans, as well as ring stones. One beautiful Roman example, dating between the 1st century BCE and 3rd century CE, is a ring stone, or seal, carved with the image of the mythical gorgon Medusa, whose visage was often worn to repel negative influences and evil intentions. This, paired with the supposed ability of peridot to do the same, makes for a rather potent symbol. In the carving, Medusa appears to be contemplating the viewer with open eyes, though when an impression is made, it's evident that her eyes are shut, seemingly sleeping, negating her fabled ability to turn others to stone with her gaze.

Though it was popular up until the end of the Roman Empire, availability of, and interest in, peridot waned for a period of nearly 1,000 years. It was not until the medieval period, when crusaders brought the stone back from the Holy Land (modern-day Israel and Palestine), that it became popular again, especially as an adornment for religious articles. These stones most likely hailed from what is now known as Pakistan, where peridot is still mined.

PHYSICAL PROPERTIES

Peridot is the gem variety of the mineral olivine, and is one of the few gemstones that occur only in one color. It is a fairly hardy gem, with a Mohs hardness of 6.5–7. There is no variety of peridot that is not some shade of green, and it owes its color to the presence of iron. Peridot is also one of only two gemstones, along with diamond, to be formed not in Earth's crust, but in the upper mantle, relying on volcanic activity to push it to the surface. Much of the peridot that makes it to Earth's surface has been damaged by its rather forceful journey from the molten rock of the upper mantle, making gem-quality peridot harder to come by than standard olivine. Despite this, peridot is not an especially rare gem, and is generally quite affordable.

MODERN-DAY SOURCES

Discoveries of peridot in Brazil by Portuguese conquistadors also rekindled an interest in the stone, which took on a fever pitch during the late-Victorian era, coinciding with the "aesthetic movement." During this time, colorful gems were paired with Renaissance-revival styles to create bright, ornate jewelry. With the discovery of large deposits of fine-quality peridot in the United States, specifically in Arizona, at the turn of the 20th century, peridot experienced yet another resurgence in popularity, and Arizona is currently the world's largest supplier of the stone, with a single location, the San Carlos Apache Reservation, providing an estimated 80–95 percent of the world's supply. The Apache Tribe has exclusive rights to mine the stone from the aptly named Peridot Mesa, and considers the stone sacred, with the power to bring rain and heal the land. Mining operations are still carried out by hand, using traditional tools, instead of large-scale mining equipment. Peridot is also found in Myanmar, China, Pakistan, and Hawaii, where it washes up on the shores of beaches in the form of pulverized sand and tiny green pebbles, generally too small for jewelry use, but prized by Hawaiians nonetheless. In Hawaiian folklore, peridot is believed to be the tears of the goddess Pele, goddess of fire and volcanoes.

PERIDOT

NOTABLE STONES

One of the most notable examples of peridot is also from the oldest known source of the stone, a cushion-cut, almost emerald-green specimen weighing just over 311 carats. Now in the collection of the Smithsonian National Museum of Natural History, it hails from the Ancient Egyptian island of Topazios itself. It is unclear when this stone was mined, but such a large specimen, hailing from a source that is now considered depleted, may well have a history dating back to at least the early 20th century.

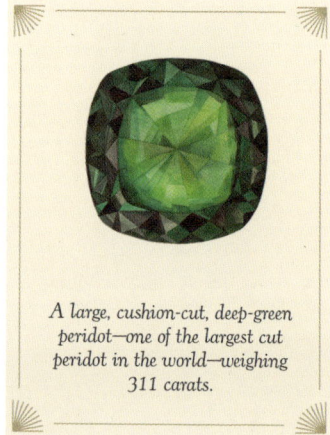

A large, cushion-cut, deep-green peridot—one of the largest cut peridot in the world—weighing 311 carats.

Given the stone's popularity during the 19th century, it is understandable that it has made a number of appearances in royal jewels. Such a bright and distinctive stone was sure to turn heads. One of the most famous sets of jewels featuring the vivid-green gem is the Hapsburg Peridot Parure, a set consisting of a large tiara, a large brooch known as a stomacher, two smaller brooches, and a rather clever necklace. The necklace has seven peridot drops that can be removed and attached to the top of the tiara, making the entire set fairly versatile, as far as giant sets of gem encrusted jewels go. The set was crafted in the 1820s for the Hapsburg family and is made with incredibly well-matched peridot leaning toward olive-green in color. Unfortunately, it seems that the parure was eventually split up, with the necklace being sold separately at auction, leaving the tiara bereft of its optional peridot drops.

The Hapsburg Peridot Parure

Though this luminous gem seems to inspire strong feelings, whether of love or distaste, it still carries a reputation for being a stone of prosperity, restful sleep, and good health. Its fiery, intense nature makes it a perennial favorite with those who enjoy vibrant sparkle in their jewelry.

Spinel

Added in 2016, the latest addition to the list of birthstones for August, brilliant and colorful spinel has an audacious history as a master of disguise. A glittering, flashing stone that comes in every color of the rainbow, spinel has long been mistaken for just about every other colored gem, and was not truly appreciated as its own stone until the advent of gemology in the 18th century. In fact, spinel itself is partially responsible for the emergence of the science of gemology, due to a desire to distinguish it from the noble and rare ruby (see Imposter Gems). As a result, there are not as many historical examples of spinel as there are other gems, but it is still a compelling and beautiful stone.

89

An octahedral spinel crystal

MISTAKEN IDENTITY

Spinel is often found in the same places as rubies and sapphires, and because of the geological conditions that create different colors of corundum, spinel found with these stones is often the same, or very similar, in color. Spinel found with ruby deposits will be colored red by chromium just as rubies are colored red by chromium, and spinel found with blue sapphire deposits will be colored blue by iron and titanium, just as blue sapphires are. This, coupled with their exceptional hardness of 7.5–8 on the Mohs scale, and absolutely brilliant shine and luster, means that they were, for a very long time, not known to be their own family of gems, leaving them rather underappreciated until very recently. Because of this confusion, many of the world's most famous rubies are, in fact, spinel! The red variety of spinel even has its own name, denoting this similarity—balas ruby—where "balas" refers to Balascia, the ancient name for Badakhshan, now part of modern-day Afghanistan, historically a source for fine-colored gems. The name "spinel" derives from the Latin word *spinella*, meaning "little spine," in reference to the crystal's pointed shape.

GROWING POPULARITY

During the 20th century, synthetic versions of spinel were used abundantly as imitations of all manner of other colored gems, leading many to associate spinel with cheap, artificial copies. But now, natural spinels are becoming increasingly sought-after. The stone does not only come in red and blue, however. It comes in practically every color imaginable for a gem, including colorless and opaque black. Because of this wide range of colors, and the stone's exceptional durability, spinel has become increasingly popular among jewelry enthusiasts and gem collectors in recent years. It also offers a seemingly endless bounty of color options to those who do not want sardonyx or peridot for the month of August.

The Bagration Spinel Tiara

Though red and blue varieties of spinel have been mistaken for ruby and sapphire in the past, other colors have been recognized as their own gem for quite a while. Purple and pink varieties were quite popular during the 19th century, possibly given a boost following the accidental discovery of the first synthetic dye in 1856, which just happened to be a deep shade of purple, called mauve. Queen Victoria, ever the trendsetter of her time, was so taken with this color that she wore a mauve dress to the 1862 International Exhibition. Empress Eugenie of France wore this fashionable new color quite often, as well. Before the discovery of this colorant, aptly named mauveine, purple dye was the rarest and most costly of all of the colors, relegating it to the wardrobes of only the rich, royalty, and the Church. Purple spinel, often exhibiting a color very close to this exciting new dye, suddenly popped up in all manner of jewelry, and remained popular into the start of the 20th century.

NOTABLE STONES

While many historical examples of spinel were originally thought to be rubies, some jewels were made in the knowledge that these stones were something unique, and different from the red rubies they have so often been mistaken for. Though there are many examples of spinel mixed in with rubies, there is one set of jewels that showcases the beauty of deep-pink spinels by themselves. This parure, known as the Bagration Spinel Parure, started off as a single tiara, made for Princess Catherine Bagration of Russia in the early 19th century. She was an incredibly controversial and emancipated woman for the time, and was known for her unconventional behavior and exceptional beauty. The initial tiara was composed of cushion-, pear-, and round-cut dark-pink spinels, set into a glittering diamond scrollwork motif. A matching comb, necklace, and a pair of earrings were later crafted to accompany the tiara, sometime during the 1840s, and set with the same dramatic, deep-pink spinels.

As one of the newest additions to the birthstone list, spinel has yet to gain as much traction as some of the "classic" stones, but it is a beautiful, brilliant gem with a broad range of gorgeous colors to choose from. There truly is something for everyone in the spinel family, whether you love it for its history as an undercover imposter or for its sheer brilliance and versatility.

SEPTEMBER

Sapphire

✳

Noble sapphire, famed for a deep-blue color
that is itself synonymous with certain shades
of blue, actually occurs in almost every color.
With a history going back to at least 800 BCE,
this durable and beautiful stone has been
treasured by many cultures and civilizations.

Sapphire

Sapphire is a variety of the mineral corundum, a very lustrous and durable stone with a hardness of 9 on the Mohs scale, just below diamond. It occurs in every color of the rainbow except red—red corundum stones are rubies. There is plenty of debate as to where on the scale from pink to red a sapphire becomes a ruby, varying by time period, location, and culture. For instance, it is possible that the Ancient Greek examples of pink sapphires would have been considered rubies at the time. What some might call a dark-pink sapphire may be considered a ruby by others, but any other color of corundum, whether colorless, black, orange, pink, blue, yellow, purple, green, or gray, is a sapphire.

THE BASICS

+ **Sapphire:** *A variety of corundum*

+ **Colors:** *All colors except red, colorless, black*

+ **Hardness:** *9*

+ **Sources:** *Myanmar, Thailand, Vietnam, Sri Lanka, Laos, Nigeria, Madagascar, Tanzania, Kenya, Afghanistan, Pakistan, Australia, Cambodia, China, Malawi, United States, Cameroon, Colombia, Ethiopia, Rwanda, India*

93

Sapphire crystals

The origins of the word "sapphire" make it clear that the earliest stones were the blue variety, with the name coming from the Ancient Greek word *sappheiros*, meaning "dark-blue stone," and likely initially referring to lapis lazuli. It is also not coincidental that the stone was associated with an ability to deflect the envy of others, as blue stones are still believed to have the power to ward off the "evil eye" in much of the Mediterranean and Middle East. It is unclear when it was known that sapphire came in colors other than blue, though there are examples of pink sapphires dating back to 300 BCE in Ancient Greece, and it is almost certain that bi-color and parti-color sapphires (stones containing two or more colors) were known in the ancient world.

SAPPHIRE MYTHOLOGY

The earliest records of sapphires date back to Ancient Persia, now modern-day Iran, where it was believed that the stone could protect from harm and envy. The Persians also believed that the world was balanced atop a giant sapphire, and that the color of the sky was a reflection of this gigantic blue gem, making it an especially important stone in their mythology. It was not only important in a spiritual sense, but sapphires were considered to be a very potent medicine, and were ground into a powder to be used in all manner of ointments and tinctures.

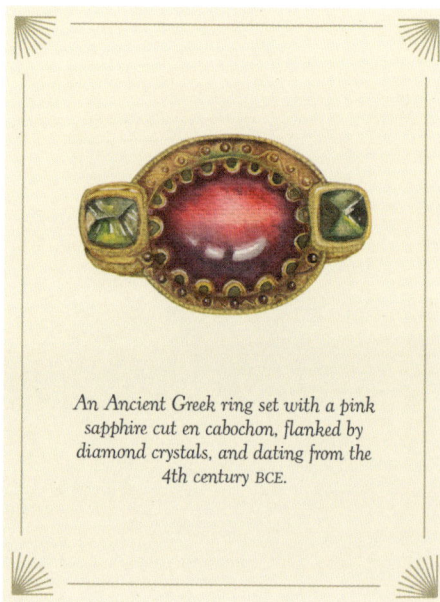

An Ancient Greek ring set with a pink sapphire cut en cabochon, flanked by diamond crystals, and dating from the 4th century BCE.

The Ancient Greeks and Romans revered the stone, also believing in its powers to prevent harm and deflect envy, as well as its ability to impart wisdom. It was even customary, in Ancient Greece, to wear a sapphire when consulting the oracles.

Ancient Hindu beliefs and Vedic astrology linked the stone to the planet Saturn, though it was thought that sapphires were not beneficial to everybody, and would bring misfortune if the stone did not suit the wearer. The Kalpavriksha, a wish-granting magical tree made of gems, supposedly had roots of sapphire. In Buddhist legends, sapphire is considered the "stone of stones," and it is thought that it can help one achieve enlightenment, as well as bring peace of mind.

ANCIENT AND MEDIEVAL APPLICATIONS

It is thought that the oldest known sapphires used in western jewelry originated from Sri Lanka, where fine sapphires and rubies are still mined today. Sri Lankan sapphires can be found in Ancient Etruscan jewelry from Italy, dating to between 600 and 275 BCE. It is not a stretch, therefore, to conclude that sapphires used by the Ancient Greeks and Romans originated in Sri Lanka, as well. The Ancient Greeks used the stones alongside other colored gems in elaborate necklaces and bracelets, as well as carved into intaglios and cameos for rings and pendants.

In the case of written records, the word *sappheiros* translating as "dark-blue stone" makes text sources difficult to trust, as it is very possible that all references to sapphires prior to the medieval era are actually referring to lapis lazuli. It is highly likely that the Ancient Greeks actually referred to sapphires using the name *hyakinthos*, the root of the word hyacinth. This stone shows up in mythology and is described as dark blue-purple, just like the hyacinth flower. In Greek myths, Hyacinth was a remarkably beautiful Spartan prince—a lover of Apollo's who was turned into the eponymous blue flower by Zeus. This connection to Apollo, the god of the Sun and patron deity of the oracles, led to sapphires being worn by those seeking the guidance and wisdom of these divine prophets.

It is said that the Pythia, the high priestess of the Temple of Apollo at Delphi, wore a sapphire on her neck when consulting the oracles that were sent to her. Knowing this, if we want to find older mentions of sapphires, we should probably look for references to a stone known as hyacinth instead. To make matters even more confusing, hyacinth (or jacinth) is a name that has also been used to refer to brown and red zircon!

An Ancient Roman carved blue-sapphire cameo depicting the goddess Venus and dating from the 1st century BCE.

Going by known sapphire artifacts, blue sapphires crop up fairly late in Ancient Greece, around the 1st century BCE. Of course, this does not mean that older examples definitely do not exist, it may simply mean that we have not found them yet. Some scholars have argued that true sapphires were unknown prior to the Roman Empire, and that all previous mentions allude

SAPPHIRE

to other blue stones, such as lapis lazuli, though the
evidence of Ancient Etruscans using Sri Lankan
sapphires, along with the Persian myth about the world
resting on a giant sapphire, and the Ancient Greek
knowledge of *hyakinthos*, all suggest otherwise.

Sapphire is one of the "cardinal" stones, alongside
diamond, emerald, and its corundum sibling, ruby.
There are references to it throughout the Bible,
though it is generally accepted that these mentions of
sappheiros once again mean lapis lazuli, not sapphire
as we know it today. Despite this, the biblical mentions
have given the stone a special place in the history of
Christianity, and sapphires were worn by members of the
clergy in medieval Europe to signify heaven, an interesting

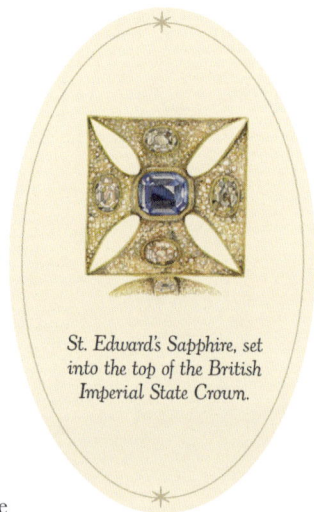

*St. Edward's Sapphire, set
into the top of the British
Imperial State Crown.*

parallel to the Ancient Persian beliefs. Around this time, sapphire also became
heavily associated with royalty, and started showing up in various crowns and royal
jewels. One stone in particular, St. Edward's Sapphire, is still part of the British
Crown Jewels, and is older than any other stone in the collection. It is thought to
date back to the 11th century, as part of a coronation ring belonging to Edward
the Confessor. Legends state that Edward, who was later canonized as a saint, was
buried with the ring upon his death in 1066, and that it was subsequently removed
from his grave when he was reinterred at Westminster Abbey in 1163. Its current
form is an octagonal rose cut, although it has almost definitely been cut multiple
times throughout its history, most recently for Charles II in the 17th century, upon
the restoration of the British monarchy. Queen Victoria had the sapphire added to
the Imperial State Crown, and it is set in the cross at the top of an almost identical
crown, known by the same name, worn by King Charles III on his coronation in
May 2023. It is thought that this lovely cornflower-blue sapphire originated in either
Afghanistan, or Sri Lanka. It is not the only sapphire in the Imperial State Crown—
the Stuart Sapphire, an impressive, deep-blue cabochon-cut oval sapphire, is set into
the bottom of the crown. It is thought that this stone dates back to King Charles II,
who reigned from 1630 to 1685.

NOTABLE SAPPHIRES

Sapphire is one of the few gemstones that can display an effect known as asterism, a phenomenon where minute inclusions inside of the stone create the illusion of a star across the top, when it is cut en cabochon. These beautiful points of light shift and move with the stone; in sapphires, the stars are always six pointed. One of the most impressive examples of star sapphires is the largest known sapphire in the world. Known as the Star of Adam, this massive, oval-shaped sapphire cabochon weighs 1,404 carats, and was found in Sri Lanka in 2015. The previous record holder for largest star sapphire, a black stone known as the Black Star of Queensland, named for its color and place of origin in Australia, is half this size, weighing 733 carats.

While the Star of Adam is the world's largest known sapphire, it is not the transparent type of stone we think of when sapphires are mentioned. The record holder for largest, cut, gem-quality sapphire is the Queen Marie of Romania Sapphire, a deep-blue stone weighing 478 carats, hailing from Sri Lanka, and originally belonging to Queen Marie of Romania. It was the centerpiece of a sautoir (a very long style of necklace) studded with diamonds and other sapphires, made by the venerable jewelry house Cartier, in 1913. Queen Marie, needing to replenish her jewels having had all of them confiscated by the Bolsheviks during the Russian Revolution, saw the necklace on display, and thought it would be a perfect match for her newly acquired sapphire tiara. After the fall of the Romanian monarchy, the necklace was sold to famed American jeweler Harry Winston, and changed hands a few more times thereafter. The necklace has since been broken up, and the lone sapphire pendant sold to a private owner, at auction, in 2003.

Another notable sapphire, known as the Logan Sapphire, is just a bit smaller at 422 carats. It is described as being the size of a chicken egg, which is a helpful reference when attempting to visualize just how large these stones are. Faceted in a beautiful, mixed cushion cut, and set into a brooch with a halo of sparkling diamonds, it, too, hails from Sri Lanka. The stone has deep-violet tones, and the cut, a rounded rectangle, is intended to enhance its color more than its brilliance. It was exhibited as a natural wonder at the 1939 New York World's Fair, and it was eventually given to the Smithsonian National Museum of Natural History by its then-owner Rebecca Guggenheim, in 1960, though it was not put on display for another decade. It is currently the largest and heaviest set gem in the museum's collection of notable, exquisite, sometimes notorious stones.

SAPPHIRE

The Star of Adam, the largest star sapphire in the world, weighing 1404.49 carats.

The Queen Marie of Romania Sapphire, the largest cut gem-quality sapphire in the world, weighing 478 carats.

The Logan Sapphire, a notably large cut sapphire the size of a chicken egg, and weighing 422 carats.

There is one more sapphire that easily dwarfs all of these stones—a mammoth, uncut sapphire crystal, also from Sri Lanka, so heavy that it is not even measured in carats. This stone, found in 2021, weighs an unprecedented 683 pounds. It has been named the Queen of Asia, and has an estimated worth of more than $100 million. Though it displays a color that is described as bluish-gray, as opposed to the deep-violet blue that is so sought after in sapphires, its size alone is enough to make up for the muted color.

PRIMARY SOURCES OF SAPPHIRES

Though Sri Lanka is the leading source of fine sapphires, it is not the only place they are found. Multiple countries in Southeast Asia produce exceptional specimens, including Myanmar, Laos, Vietnam, and Thailand. Africa also boasts some productive sapphire deposits, especially in colors other than blue, notably in Tanzania, Madagascar, Nigeria, and Kenya. Afghanistan, Pakistan, and the region of Kashmir, in India, have unique corundum deposits, with beautiful bright rubies and sapphires alike, and Australia has been a source of sapphires since the middle of the 1800s. One of the most recent, and more interesting, sources of sapphires is the state of Montana in the United States. Initially discovered by gold prospectors mining for gold in the Missouri River in the 1860s, the stones were thought to be worthless. They were often discarded, and were even seen as a nuisance for clogging up gold-mining equipment. They were not considered valuable until a few decades later. What makes Montana sapphires unique is their relatively small size—most rough stones are no larger than a pebble—and their candy-colored pastel palette. These stones tend to be lighter colored than other sapphires, though richer, deeper blues, greens, and teals do exist.

While the early history of sapphires is a bit murky, due to the different names given to the stone through the ages, it remains one of the most popular gems on the market. While blue will always be the most sought-after color, there is a growing desire for the beautiful range of rainbow colors that sapphires can be found in, making this a stone that has the potential to appeal to just about anyone. In keeping with the ancient traditions regarding the stone, it is still believed to be a symbol of knowledge and wealth, and as a protection for the wearer from envy.

OCTOBER

Opal - Tourmaline

✳

While many birthstones come in a range of colors, there are none that are as colorful within a single specimen as opal, the traditional birthstone for October. In 1952, this month was given a second birthstone, tourmaline. Initially, it was specifically pink tourmaline that was added to the list, but it has become increasingly common to embrace all of its stunning shades as birthstones for October.

Opal

Pieces of mineralogical magic, opals display a shifting, twinkling, rainbow of colors, against an opaque, translucent—or sometimes transparent—background and, like so many gemstones, they have an incredibly long history of use in adornments.

The earliest recorded stones date back to Slovakian opal mines, around 400 BCE. These mines were not only the oldest known source, but were also the world's only source of opal until deposits were "discovered" in Mexico, by Spanish conquistadors, in the early 16th century. The Slovenian opal mines were in almost continuous operation until 1922, when mining finally ceased. They provided beautiful shimmering gemstones for more than 2,000 years. By then, the majority of the world's opals were being mined in Australia, after their "discovery" in 1849 (they had been in use by the Indigenous populations of Australia for far longer—likely for thousands of years before British colonization). Australian opal mines account for about 95 percent of the world's opal production today, though significant amounts are also mined in Mexico, Ethiopia (where deposits were found in the early 1990s), Brazil, and the western United States.

THE BASICS

+ **Opal:** A silicate mineral

+ **Colors:** White, colorless, pink, red, blue, yellow, red, orange, green, brown

+ **Hardness:** 5.5–6.5

+ **Sources:** Australia, Mexico, Brazil, Honduras, Turkey, Czech Republic, Canada, Slovakia, Hungary, Indonesia, Ethiopia, Guatemala, Nicaragua

101

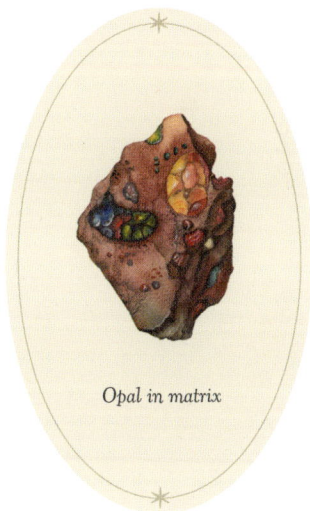

Opal in matrix

CULTURAL SIGNIFICANCE

It is very likely that the Ancient Egyptians and Babylonions were some of the first cultures to use opals in their jewelry and adornments, fashioning them into protective amulets and talismans. Both cultures considered the stone to have protective powers, and to bring the wearer great luck and fortune. Ancient Greeks believed that the stone not only protected from disease, but gave the wearer the gift of prophecy and foresight. They believed the stone was formed by the tears of Zeus, god of lightning, after his defeat of the mighty Titans. Similarly, Ancient Arabic legends state that opals were born of lightning flashes. It is not difficult to see why this stone would be associated with lightning, since it seemingly encapsulates flashes of light. The Ancient Romans had a particular love for opal, considering it an especially lucky stone, as well as a symbol of hope and purity. They referred to the stone as "Cupid's stone," believing that opals could rekindle love, and associated them not only with Cupid, but also with Venus, goddess of love and beauty. The name "opal" itself likely harkens back to Ancient Rome, when it was called *opalus*, from the Greek *opallios*, both meaning "to see a change of color." It has also been suggested that the Greek word *opallios* originally came from the ancient Sanskrit word *upalos*, meaning "precious stone."

While Spanish Conquistadors brought Mexican opal back to Europe as part of the riches they stole from the Americas, there is archaeological evidence to suggest that the Mexica people were mining and using the stone as early as 850 CE. A particular variety of opal, found in abundance in Mexico and known as fire opal, was especially significant to the Mexica people, and was used in religious and ceremonial objects. Opal was thought to represent joy, life, abundance, and divinity, being given the name *huitzitziltecpatl* (stone like a bird of a thousand colors) in the Nahuatl language. Indigenous cultures in what is now the Republic of Honduras were also mining and using opal well before Europeans showed up. The Indigenous cultures of Australia believed, and still do believe, that opals are a sacred link between the earthly and the divine, and a gateway to the ancestral realms. Indigenous Australians likely considered opal outcrops to be sacred for thousands of years before their "discovery" and subsequent mining by British colonizers.

NEGATIVE MYTHOLOGY

It may surprise some people to read that opal has such a long reputation as a stone of good fortune, because it has spent the last two centuries being regarded as a rather unlucky gem. This unfortunate reputation can be traced back to a single book, Sir Walter Scott's 1829 novel *Anne of Geierstein*. In this book, a demoness is killed when holy water is spilled on her opal, and the general public interpreted this as a warning about the bad luck that would befall those who wear opals. The unlucky nature of opals has been interpreted multiple ways—that opals are unlucky unless they are your birthstone; that engagement rings should never contain opals; and that an opal received as a gift will bring bad luck unless it also involves at least a small sum of money changing hands so that it becomes a financial transaction, instead. Needless to say, none of these myths are true, but the popularity of both the book and the ensuing ideas about opals bringing bad fortune essentially crashed the opal market. One influential opal lover in particular was especially upset about this mythology— the trendsetter of her time, British Queen Victoria. She took it upon herself to try to reverse public opinion about the stone, both wearing and gifting opals at every occasion. Two of her five daughters went on to marry, and both received a suite of opal jewelry as wedding gifts. Those who looked to Queen Victoria for guidance on what was in and what was out believed that opals could not be unlucky if she were gifting them to such important loved ones, for such an important occasion. Her campaign to end the stigma surrounding opals seems to have been at least partially successful, though the myths about unfortunate opals persist today.

OPAL

PHYSICAL PROPERTIES

Unlike other gems, which are minerals with a defined crystalline structure, opal is technically a mineraloid, an amorphous form of silica bearing a rather significant amount of water. Displaying reflective flashes of every color of the rainbow, opals can have a background (matrix) of white, black, gray, yellow, orange, red, or completely colorless and transparent. Opals usually contain between 6 and 10 percent water, which puts them at risk of drying out and cracking if they are not stored properly. This quality, coupled with the fact that they are rather soft—between 5 and 6.5 on the Mohs scale—means they are one of the more fragile gems, and accounts for the lack of ancient artifacts made of opal. For an ancient piece of opal to have survived to the modern age, it would have to have been kept in ideal conditions, with the right amount of ambient humidity, as well as no danger of breakage. One of the oldest known opals dates to between 500 and 700 CE, originating in the Byzantine era, and is a tiny stone set in an elaborate gold and gem-studded bracelet, likely made in what was then known as Constantinople, now Istanbul. The bracelet is one of a pair, currently in the collection of New York's Metropolitan Museum of Art. That the stone has survived intact within the bracelet seems rather miraculous, considering it is the only one of three opals in the bracelet that remains (and because this bracelet is one of a pair, it is one of six original opals to have remained in the set). The diminutive size of this opal, compared to the larger colored gems and pearls set into both bracelets, hints at the value and rarity of the stone at the time.

The Flame Queen opal, an incredibly unusual opal displaying a rare effect known as "eye-of-opal."

NOTABLE OPALS

Because Australia is the source of so much of the
opal on the market, it is no surprise that the largest
known opal was found there. A hefty stone weighing
17,000 carats, the Olympic Australis was discovered
in 1956, in Coober Pedy, a town sometimes referred
to as "the opal capital of the world." Despite
having the potential to be cut into more than 10,000
individual, one-carat stones, the giant opal has been
left uncut, and is estimated to be worth more than
$1.5 million. Another striking and unusual specimen
is known as the Flame Queen opal, and it displays a
rare effect known as "eye-of-opal," which occurs when a
cavity in a rock is filled in with opal over time. In the case of the
Flame Queen, there are two layers of opal, creating the illusion of an outer ring and
inner "eye." This incredible stone was discovered in 1906, and though it was initially
sold by the men who found it for just $125, it was eventually purchased by J. D.
Rockefeller in the 1940s for more than $95,000.

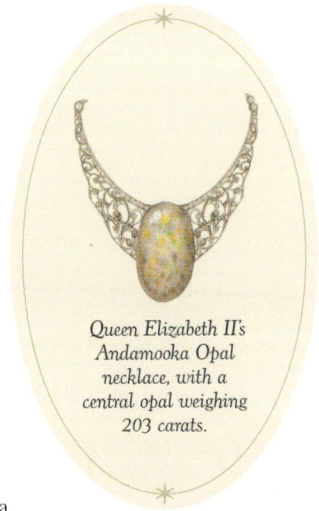

*Queen Elizabeth II's
Andamooka Opal
necklace, with a
central opal weighing
203 carats.*

Of all of the famous pieces of opal jewelry, there is one that stands out for its sheer
size alone—the Andamooka Opal, also known as the Queen's Opal. A vibrant, fiery
opal with a weight of 203 carats, this captivating oval stone was presented to Queen
Elizabeth II in 1954, to mark the occasion of her first visit to South Australia. It was
subsequently set into a necklace made of diamonds and palladium, along with a
matching pair of earrings, though it was only worn once before being placed into the
royal vaults.

Despite having a lingering reputation for bringing bad luck to those who wear it,
opals have remained an enduring favorite among jewelry lovers and gem collectors
alike. The gem's ability to captivate the imagination with its brilliant flashes of color
has not diminished over time, and it is still considered as beautiful and special as it
was in the ancient world. The tide of public opinion regarding opals seems to be
shifting, with more people purchasing and gifting opals despite the centuries of bad
press, and the discovery of large quantities of opals in Ethiopia in the 1990s have
made the stone far more affordable and accessible to those who wish to own a little
piece of solid lightning.

Tourmaline

Perhaps because of the negative associations surrounding giving gifts of opals, but more likely because of concerns about durability, October was given a second birthstone in 1952, the colorful and versatile tourmaline.

A STONE OF MANY COLORS

Tourmaline has a very long history, but because of its wide array of hues, it has often been mistaken for other gems, much like one of August's birthstones, spinel. Even the name "tourmaline" hints at this confusion, stemming from the Sinhalese word *toramalli*, which means "stone of mixed colors," but was originally used to refer to an entirely different stone, carnelian. Tourmaline comes in the same color as just about every other gemstone—there is even a variety known as "rubellite" because of its uncanny resemblance to ruby.

Not only does tourmaline come in a staggering range of hues, it often displays more than one color per stone. Some of the best-known varieties of tourmaline are those famous for this effect, such as watermelon tourmaline, which, like the fruit it is named for, displays a "rind" of green around a core of pink or red.

Tourmaline crystal

THE BASICS

+ **Tourmaline:** *A group of crystalline silicate minerals*

+ **Colors:** *All colors, including black and colorless*

+ **Hardness:** 7–7.5

+ **Sources:** *Afghanistan, Pakistan, United States, Brazil, Tanzania, Nigeria, Kenya, Indonesia, Sri Lanka, India, Madagascar, Mozambique, Malawi, Namibia*

106

A PATCHY PAST

Ancient examples of tourmaline exist, but they were almost certainly thought to be different stones entirely. It was not until the 18th century, with the advent of gemology as a science, that tourmaline was discovered to be a gemstone in its own right. Before this time, the only variety of tourmaline that was recognized as its own distinct stone was black tourmaline, which was known as schorl as early as the 15th century. Unfortunately, this murky history leaves us without any ancient or older historical beliefs regarding the stone

An Ancient Greek carved tourmaline seal featuring an image of Alexander the Great. Dating from the 4th century BCE, it is the oldest known carved tourmaline in the world.

The oldest known tourmaline artifact does, in fact, date back to Ancient Greece. It is a carved intaglio portrait of Alexander the Great from the 4th century BCE, made of bi-color gold and red tourmaline. It is hard to say exactly what gem the Ancient Greeks thought this was, but it was clearly highly regarded, judging by the subject matter and quality of the carving. Other notable historical examples of tourmaline were originally thought to be different stones, such as emerald and ruby. One such example is a large red tourmaline in a 14th-century crown known as the Crown of St. Wenceslas. Made in 1346, the crown is set with large blue sapphires and emeralds, as well as a handful of spinels and a central rubellite tourmaline—this and the spinels were both thought to be rubies at the time the crown was crafted. (For more notable tourmalines that were mistaken for other gems, see Imposter Gems.)

While we may not have ancient myths and beliefs surrounding tourmaline, we do know how people felt about the stone during the Renaissance, and later. By the early 1700s, it had become clear that some of the colorful gems being brought back from Sri Lanka by Dutch traders were not, in fact, zircon, as had been suspected, but an entirely different kind of stone. This led to a vogue for multicolored tourmaline among the wealthy and the nobility throughout Europe. The colorful nature of the stone led to it being associated with artistic ability and creativity, giving it a reputation as a stone that would bring inspiration. It is now also considered a stone of healing, reconciliation, and is thought to promote emotional balance.

107

SOURCES OF TOURMALINE

In the centuries since tourmaline gained its independence as a gem, it has been found in many places around the world. Though the majority of it is mined in Brazil and multiple African countries today, it is also abundant in less expected places, such as the small Italian island of Elba, for which the variety of tourmaline elbaite is named. Tourmaline has also been found in large quantities in the United States, with pink tourmaline from California having been a particular favorite of the Chinese Empress Dowager Cixi during the late 1800s. The state of Maine also produces beautiful and unusual colors of tourmaline—so much so that it is the official state stone. Fine-quality stones are also mined in Pakistan, Afghanistan, India, Sri Lanka, and Indonesia.

A bright-blue faceted Brazilian paraiba tourmaline

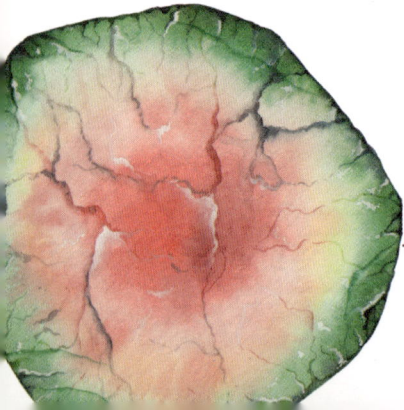

NOTABLE VARIETIES

Some of the most sensational examples of tourmaline are valued for their unique color, not necessarily their size. While you can find tourmaline in every hue, there is one, in particular, that is prized more than any other: bright-blue paraíba. Found only in a small region of Brazil, for which the tourmaline is named, these neon-blue stones derive their color from large quantities of copper. It gives them an otherworldly, vibrant glow that is truly unmatched in any other gem. Paraíba tourmaline is a fairly recent discovery, having been found in the late 1980s. Interest in the new and unusual stone was immediately apparent, with prices ballooning following its discovery. After initially selling for $200 per carat, stones easily exceed $50,000 per carat today. Supplies of Brazilian paraíba tourmaline are incredibly limited, but similar, if slightly less-saturated, varieties have been found on the coast of Nigeria, exactly where the continents of South America and Africa would have lined up in the distant past when all of Earth's continents formed the giant landmass known as Pangea. Bright-blue tourmalines of similar color have also been found in Mozambique, but they contain their own trace elements in addition to copper, and are not as vibrant as the stones from Brazil or Nigeria. Other stunning examples of tourmaline are prized for the number of colors evident in one specimen, with some tourmaline crystals showing upward of 10 colors.

Though tourmaline may lack the ancient history of so many other gemstones, it is becoming an increasingly popular choice for fine jewelry enthusiasts and gem lovers alike. Whatever your favorite color may be, there is a tourmaline out there in that color. There is probably even a tourmaline out there in a combination of all your favorite colors!

NOVEMBER

Topaz - Citrine

✳

November has the peculiar distinction of having
two birthstones that look almost identical. The
golden-yellow variety of topaz was extremely
popular when the first official list of birthstones
was made in 1912. The second stone for this
month, citrine, was added along with the first
set of changes to the birthstone list, in 1952.

Topaz

On paper, topaz seems to have a fairly ancient history, showing up in the writings of Ancient Egypt, Greece, and Rome, but unfortunately, this is an unreliable history.

UNCERTAIN ORIGINS

The name "topaz" comes from the word *topazios*, and despite some sources claiming that this has always been the name for this stone, it is clear that this was the name once given to an entirely different gem—namely, bright-green peridot and the yellow variety of the same mineral, chrysolite.

+ **Topaz:** *A silicate mineral*

+ **Colors:** *Yellow, orange, red, pink, blue, brown, purple, colorless, black*

+ **Hardness:** *8*

+ **Sources:** *Russia, Brazil, Mexico, United States, Myanmar, Namibia, Zimbabwe, Madagascar, Sri Lanka, Pakistan, China, Australia*

111

A topaz crystal

Topazios Island, a small volcanic island in the Red Sea, now known as Zabargad Island, was the ancient source of peridot and chrysolite. Much like sapphire, with its muddled history and multiple names (including yellow sapphire, also at one time called topaz), an inability to pinpoint exactly which stone is being referred to in ancient sources makes it hard to know just how long topaz has been known and used as a gemstone. In much the same way that ruby once referred to all dark-pink and deep-red gems, topaz seems to have been a catch-all name for all manner of yellow gemstones.

The more recent, and more verifiable, history of topaz dates back to its discovery in Germany in 1737. This is the first time that the name "topaz" is applied to this specific mineral, though it is unclear why it was suddenly applied to this stone, and not all yellow stones, as in the past. At nearly the same time, in 1735, large deposits of topaz were discovered in Brazil by Portuguese colonists. One of the spoils of colonialism, the first stones to be found were sent back to the Portuguese royal court, which accounts for the name "imperial" topaz. It seems that misidentification is a recurring theme in the story of topaz, as one of the first large gems sent back to Portugal was thought to be a huge diamond. Now lost to time, it was set into a royal crown. The German topaz deposits were the primary source of the gem for Europe until 1768, when the Portuguese officially recognized the Brazilian topaz deposits as commercially significant, and large-scale mining began; Brazil still provides the majority of the world's topaz today. From here, interest in the stone blossomed, with topaz becoming a favorite gem during the late 1700s through the 1800s. It is highly likely that any topaz predating discoveries in Germany and Brazil came from Sri Lanka, the source of so many incredible gems throughout history.

Deposits of the imperial variety were found in Russia, in the Ural Mountains, in the 19th century, and this was another significant source of the stone for much of Europe. The discovery of irradiation and heat-treatment to create vibrant blue stones once again revived interest in topaz in the 1960s, and the heat-treated blue variety has remained popular ever since. Subsequent discoveries of topaz deposits around the world have created more knowledge—and demand—for colors beyond the famed golden yellow, peachy pink, and bright blue. Aside from Brazil, topaz is now mined in Mexico, Australia, the United States, and Zimbabwe, one of the only sources of naturally occurring vibrant blue topaz (though it is much paler than heat-treated varieties).

ANCIENT SYMBOLISM

Though the ancient history of topaz is difficult to separate from that of other yellow stones, we do know what beliefs were attributed to the large family of yellow gems under the umbrella of "topaz." Ancient Greeks believed that the stone could grant the wearer strength, and potentially, the power of invisibility in times of need. Ancient Romans thought that it provided protection while traveling, and that placing topaz near food could cause the stone to change color if the food was poisoned. In Renaissance Europe, it was thought that topaz could soothe anger, as well as break magic spells. Nowadays, topaz is regarded as a stone with the ability to attract wealth, and as a symbol of love and affection.

TOPAZ COLORS

The variety of topaz known as "imperial," or "precious," topaz is golden-yellow to peachy-pink. This may seem surprising in light of the blue variety that has flooded the jewelry market since the 1960s. The discovery that colorless topaz could be irradiated, and then heat-treated, to create blue stones led various shades of blue topaz to dominate the jewelry world, quickly becoming very affordable and accessible gems. Despite the profusion of heat-treated blue topaz, and the emphasis on golden topaz throughout history, it is a stone that comes in a wide range of colors. The most common variety is colorless, but topaz can also occur in all shades of pink, red, orange, brown, green, gray, and purple, as well as pale blues (not to be confused with the vibrant blues of heat-treated topaz).

TOPAZ

NOTABLE SPECIMENS

Though notable examples of other gemstones are prized for their large size, they do not come close to the largest topaz specimens. Topaz stones are often free of inclusions and imperfections, and therefore completely clear. Coupled with the large size of some of these stones, this makes them especially impressive. The largest cut topaz, known as the El Dorado Topaz, also happens to be the largest cut gem in the world. Hailing from the Minas Gerais region of Brazil, it has a smoky, yellow-gray color, and weighs 31,000 carats, and was cut from a single crystal initially weighing 81.5lb (37kg). The El Dorado Topaz is privately owned, but is on public display in Madrid, Spain. Another massive specimen, the American Golden Topaz, weighs just over 22,892.5 carats, and is a pale, lemon-yellow color. This stone, held in the collection of the Smithsonian National Museum of Natural History, also hails from the Minas Gerais region of Brazil. While these two stones are notable for their enormous size and clarity, there is yet another specimen, nowhere near as massive, that is famed for its incredible, vibrant red color. Known as the Whitney Flame Topaz, and also to be found at the Smithsonian, this 48.86-carat stone displays a deep, fuchsia-red color generally associated with rubies. Entirely untreated, and also hailing from Minas Gerais, it represents the rarest color of topaz, as well as one of the rarest gems in the Smithsonian's collection.

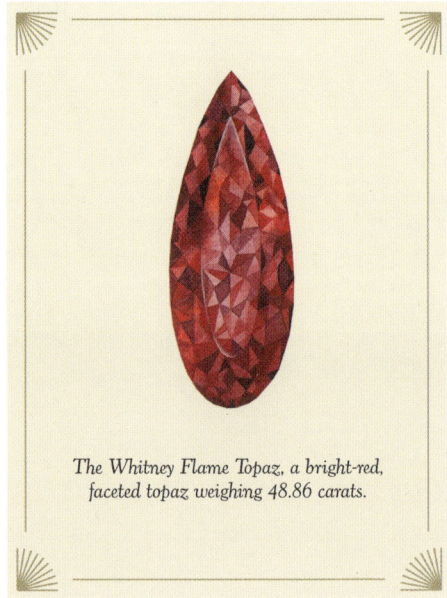

The Whitney Flame Topaz, a bright-red, faceted topaz weighing 48.86 carats.

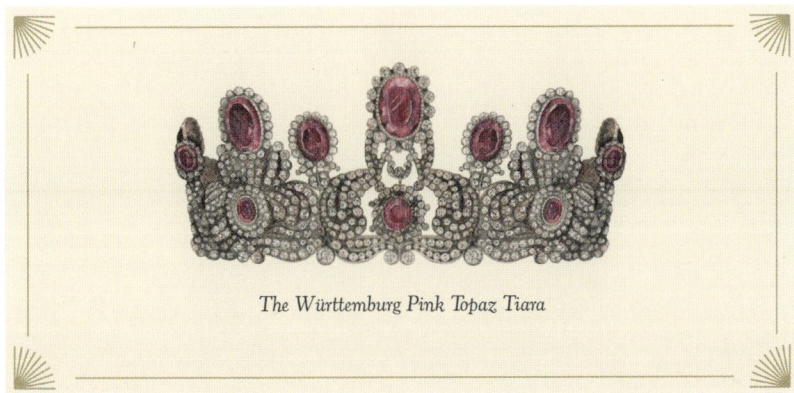

The Württemburg Pink Topaz Tiara

The rarity of pink and red topaz, even more coveted than the gold variety, has made it a natural fit for royal jewels. There was a vogue for pink topaz jewels among European royalty in the 19th century, with a few exceptional examples surviving to the modern day. One set of pink topaz jewelry that is still worn today is known as the Württemburg Pink Topaz Parure. Crafted sometime during the first half of the 19th century, it was purchased by Tsar Nicholas I of Russia as a gift for his daughter Olga, who would go on to become the queen of Württemburg. The parure consists of a topaz-and-diamond tiara, a necklace, bracelets, earrings, and a brooch, all set with matching, deep-pink topaz. The set is now owned by Charlotte Henrietta de Rothschild, of the famed Rothschild family. A renowned soprano, she has worn the tiara and various pieces of the parure for multiple performances.

Citrine

The addition of citrine to November's birthstones in 1952 was likely spurred on by the fact that it so closely resembles topaz as to be nearly impossible for the casual observer to tell them apart. The stone can be created by heat-treating other varieties of quartz, such as amethyst and smoky quartz, leading to a more accessible and affordable stone with the look of golden topaz.

Naturally occurring citrine does exist, but it is fairly rare, with more than 95 percent of commercially available citrine starting out as amethyst or smoky quartz. Because of its similarity to topaz, and the fact that both "topaz" and "citrine" were words used to describe all manner of yellow stones, citrine's history is as unclear as that of topaz, and the two are intricately intertwined. If citrine was used in the ancient world—and it most certainly was—it would most likely have been known as yellow quartz.

116

THE BASICS

+ **Citrine:** *A variety of quartz*

+ **Colors:** *Yellow, orange, red, pink, blue, brown, purple, colorless, black*

+ **Hardness:** *8*

+ **Sources:** *Brazil, Bolivia, United States, Madagascar, Russia, France, Democratic Republic of the Congo, China, Spain, Uruguay, Zambia*

This carved citrine fish intaglio from Ancient Greece is one of the oldest examples of cut citrine, dating from the 5th century BCE.

ANCIENT EXAMPLES

Though citrine was almost certainly known before the time of Ancient Greece, the oldest known examples of citrine being used in jewelry date from that time period. Carved seals and intaglios, intended to be worn as rings or pendants, bore the images of mythological heroes, or symbols of abundance and fertility, such as fish. The Greeks, keenly observant and skilled masters of stone carving, must have realized that this yellow stone shared many of the same properties as other forms of quartz, such as rock crystal and amethyst.

One of the oldest examples of citrine as adornment can be attributed to the Ancient Greeks—an open-mouthed fish carved into a very pale, yellow citrine, dating to the 5th century BCE. Carrying on the tradition of carving images into gems, the Ancient Romans left behind many examples of citrine intaglios. A beautiful carved intaglio seal of Bonus Eventus (the personification of success) dating to the 1st century CE is a testament to the stone's use and symbolism in the ancient world, though what the Romans would have called it, we can only guess. The Romans believed the stone could shield the wearer from evil thoughts, and in medieval Europe, the Celts and Scots believed the stone could protect against the plague.

A carved citrine intaglio from Ancient Rome. It depicts the personification of success, Bonus Eventus, and dates from the 1st century CE.

SOURCES AND PHYSICAL PROPERTIES

The name "citrine" hints at its sunny color, stemming from *citron*, the French word for lemon. Known in the past as the "merchant's stone," citrine was thought to attract wealth and prosperity, due to it being the color of gold. Scotland has a lengthy history of citrine mining. A particularly lovely variety of dark-orange citrine, known as Cairngorm can be found in the Scottish mountain range of the same name, and became particularly popular during the Victorian era (mostly because, like so many things that became trendy during this time, Queen Victoria herself was very fond of it). The discovery of citrine deposits by European colonists, in both Bolivia and Brazil, in the 16th century, created a new demand for a stone that, until then, had been exceptionally rare. The discovery that other varieties of quartz could be heat-treated to create citrine, likely in the 18th century, made the sunny yellow stone even more accessible and affordable, after a long history of being hard to acquire.

117

NOTABLE GEMS

Citrine is not known for having exceptionally large crystals. They usually occur in geodes, which do not yield very large stones. Despite this, the world's largest cut citrine, known as the Malaga Citrine, is nearly as large as some of the world's largest topaz, and happens to be owned by the same group that owns the enormous El Dorado Topaz. The Malaga is a pale-yellow, faceted oval, free of visible inclusions, and weighs an impressive 20,200 carats. Like the unbelievably large topaz specimens that boast the title of largest cut gems, this sunny yellow citrine hails from the Minas Gerais region of Brazil. Before it was discovered, the previous record holder for largest citrine was a stone known as the Sol del Sur, not quite as large as the Malaga, but still weighing a respectable 8,200 carats. Both of these stones represent anomalies in the citrine world, and are true rarities—for their exceptional clarity as well as massive size. They are also both owned by the same private group, and were, until fairly recently, on display in Spain.

Some of the most impressive citrines are not notable for their size, but for their rarity, having been fashioned at a time when sourcing the stone would have been fairly difficult. One such example is a pendant bearing a carved portrait of King Philip II of Spain. Created sometime in the mid-1550s, this specimen certainly predates the knowledge of heat-treating other varieties of quartz to create citrine. It is very likely that this citrine represents one of the earliest stones to come from colonial mines in South America, though whether it came from Bolivia, still one of the world's leading producers of citrine, or Brazil, is unknown. The exquisitely carved Renaissance gem can be found at the Cleveland Museum of Art. Another exceptional citrine—tied not to a monarch, but to Hollywood royalty—is a modern necklace known as the Jolie Citrine Necklace. Designed, and donated to the Smithsonian National Museum of Natural History, by actress Angelina Jolie, the centerpiece of the necklace is a deep orange-brown pear-shaped citrine weighing 177 carats. This stone is notable not only for its famous namesake, but for the luxurious, deep-orange color of the stone, a shade often referred to as "madeira."

Whether preferring the rainbow hues of topaz, or the sunny yellows of citrine, November's birthstones afford gem lovers a wealth of options. Though the histories of both stones may be a little unclear, and coincidentally, intertwined, they are both beautiful gems that offer jewelry lovers and gem collectors a spectrum of colors (and price points) to choose from. If vibrant stones are favored, heat-treated blue topaz and amethyst-turned-citrine both qualify, while untreated topaz and citrine boast a bevy of rare, exceptional options for those who prefer their stones to be colored only by nature.

The Jolie Citrine Necklace, designed by Angelina Jolie and now part of the collection of the Smithsonian National Museum of Natural History.

A carved citrine intaglio portrait of King Philip II of Spain dating from the 1550s.

DECEMBER

Turquoise - Zircon - Tanzanite

✳

Ending the year with a rich variety of options,
December is both the last month of the calendar year,
and the third month with three birthstone options,
traditionally all shades of blue: turquoise, zircon,
and tanzanite. Though all three share a common
color, they have very different histories, spanning
from some of the earliest examples of gemstones
used for human adornment (turquoise), to one of
the most recently discovered gems (tanzanite).

Turquoise

The original stone for this month is one so blue that its name is synonymous with a color—vibrant, timeless turquoise. With a history spanning thousands of years, across many cultures throughout the entire world, turquoise is a universally beloved stone that has been significant as both a form of adornment and a source of pigment.

The oldest known turquoise artifacts date back to the 6th millennium BCE, and were found in two very different locations, Egypt and Bulgaria. The Egyptian finds consist of fragments of high-quality turquoise, found in tombs dating back to around 5000 BCE, while the Bulgarian finds are shaped turquoise beads, from roughly the same time period. Some scholars have put forth the theory that turquoise is the oldest known gem, and given the evidence, it does not seem a very far-fetched idea.

The color of turquoise offers a clue as to why it has been in use for so long. Deriving its blue shades from an abundance of copper, it is often found within, or very close to, copper mines. Given that humans have been mining copper for roughly ten thousand years, ancient people were bound to find a use for the bright blue stones that turned up when digging for copper ore. However, finer, gem-quality turquoise is more often found independent of copper deposits.

THE BASICS

+ **Turquoise:** A hydrous phosphate of copper and aluminum

+ **Colors:** Light to dark blue, green, white

+ **Hardness:** 5–6

+ **Sources:** United States, China, Iran, Egypt, Chile, Afghanistan, Brazil, Armenia, Australia, Israel, Kazakhstan

A large turquoise nugget

LOW-QUALITY TURQUOISE

Gem-quality stones are actually rather rare, as the conditions required for them to form are fairly specific: turquoise forms when acidic groundwater comes into contact with copper, usually at higher elevations of 3,000– 8,500ft (900–2,500m). The seemingly endless availability of turquoise in our modern world can be attributed to a few things. The first is the practice of stabilizing lower-quality turquoise—soft, chalky, less desirable material is treated to increase its hardness and color saturation. There is also reconstituted turquoise, where ground-up fragments and powder from lower-quality material are mixed with various resins and binders, and pressed to create a facsimile of gem-quality turquoise. Worst of all is the dyeing of other, unrelated minerals, such as howlite, or even plastics. These are often sold as turquoise without any disclaimer. Often, it is hard for the casual jewelry lover to distinguish between these subpar materials and true, gem-quality turquoise, though price can sometimes be an indicator. Ancient cultures would have likely scoffed at the profusion of "fake" turquoise that floods the jewelry market today.

ANCIENT HISTORY

It seems that every culture that has encountered turquoise has considered it very significant, with legends and symbolism surrounding the stone being found in Persia (modern-day Iran), Ancient Egypt, Ancient Greece, Ancient Rome, China, Mesopotamia, and the Americas.

Turquoise was precious to the Ancient Persians, and remains a highly regarded stone in modern-day Iran. Persian turquoise, noted for its vibrant, robin's-egg-blue color with very few visible veins, was connected with the purity of the heavens. The Persians called the stone *piruzeh*, and associated it with victory, prosperity, and protection from danger. Archaeological discoveries in this part of the world seem to suggest that turquoise was being mined as far back as 7000 BCE. The trade of turquoise was an important part of the Persian economy for thousands of years, finding its way farther west, and south, via the Silk Road, a network of trade routes connecting the Middle East and Asia with Europe and the Mediterranean. This trade route is likely responsible for the modern name "turquoise," which comes from the French words *pierre turquoise*, meaning "Turkish stone," and ties in with the mistaken belief that the stone originated in Turkey. Though the stone has been prized there for centuries, it was not its source but simply a stop along the Silk Road before heading farther west to Europe.

DECEMBER

The Ancient Egyptians called the stone *mefkat*, which means "joy" or "delight," and it was closely associated with the goddess of joy, the sky, and fertility, Hathor. They believed turquoise to be a protective stone, and it was particularly prized for use in royal regalia. The favored Egyptian color combination of orange-red, dark blue, and light, blue-green could only have been achieved with turquoise (carnelian and often made up the other two colors), and despite the prevalence of turquoise-colored inlay and beads in jewelry, masks, and other burial goods, true turquoise was actually a rarity. Modern reassessments of turquoise-colored gems and beads in Egyptian artifacts in museum collections have found that quite a few of these are, in fact, glass or faience (a type of glazed earthenware) made to look like turquoise, further underscoring its value to the Ancient Egyptians. Turquoise was mined on the Sinai Peninsula, in Egypt, but was (and continues to be) in rather scarce supply. Sinai turquoise tends to exhibit a translucence that is fairly rare for the stone. Despite this scarcity, turquoise powder was also used as pigment, especially important for achieving the vibrant blues seen in the frescoes in Ancient Egyptian tombs.

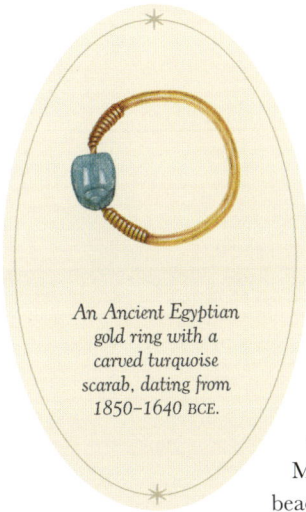

An Ancient Egyptian gold ring with a carved turquoise scarab, dating from 1850–1640 BCE.

123

The Ancient Greeks and Romans shared similar beliefs about turquoise, likely influenced by older civilizations such as the Persians and Egyptians. They believed the stone could protect not only from harm, but from the evil eye—a belief still commonly ascribed to blue stones, especially in the Mediterranean and Middle East. They also believed that the stone could bring good fortune to those who wore it. In Ancient Tibet, the stone was regarded as the "sky stone," and has been in use since at least 1000 BCE. Turquoise has been used as a form of currency in Tibet for millenia, and it is separated into six grades, according to value, with the most valuable being worth more than gold. Turquoise is still an integral and important part of Tibetan culture.

Reverence of this bright-blue stone was also prevalent in the pre-Columbian cultures of the Americas. It was considered a sacred stone by Mesoamerican cultures such as the Maya and Mexica, used in jewelry as well as sacred ceremonial objects such as masks. The Mexica associated the stone with fire, and were known to separate and

TURQUOISE

A turquoise mosaic mask of Xiuhtecuhtli, the Mexica god of fire, daytime, and heat, dating from 1400–1521 CE.

name different grades of turquoise based on quality and purpose. *Xihuitl* was the name given to the less valuable, more common, variety, used for mosaics and inlays, whereas *teoxihuitl* was considered to be closely tied to the divine, and highly prized for its beauty. The word *xihuitl* also meant "year," and turquoise was associated with Xiuhtecuhtli, the god of both time and fire. Though the Maya and Mexica would have mined much of their own turquoise close to home, it is very likely that some of the turquoise used in Mesoamerica was actually mined in, and traded from, the American Southwest, still one of the top sources of turquoise today. Archaeological evidence, as well as ancestral tradition, show that turquoise was being mined by the ancient Puebloan and Hohokam tribes of the American Southwest as early as 200 BCE. These tribes believed that turquoise could bring health, happiness, and good fortune, and it was an important component of their sacred ceremonies.

NOTABLE STONES

Today, the United States is the world's largest supplier of turquoise, with much of the mined material coming from Arizona. Given the abundance of material coming out of the United States, it is not a surprise that some of the world's largest known turquoise nuggets have been found there, though at these sizes it would be more accurate to call them boulders. One such stone is a massive 555,651-carat stone, mined in 1982, at the Mona Lisa mine in Arkansas. It is a pale, sky blue with rich red veins running through it. The record holder for absolute largest turquoise slab ever found comes from China, also a source for very fine stones, and it is nearly double the size of the largest American turquoise, at 1,124,909 carats. It is currently on display at the Shandong Tianyu Museum of Natural History in Linyi, China. Though the United States and China are two of the main sources of turquoise, it is also mined in Egypt, at its ancient source in the Sinai Peninsula, as well as Kazakhstan, Iran, and Mexico.

Zircon

Despite being a stone known since ancient times, with a rich history and a rainbow of colors, zircon has the unfortunate burden of being confused with cubic zirconia, the widely available, synthetic diamond simulant that began dominating lower-priced jewelry in the late 20th century. Due to this confusion, zircon is not as popular as it once was, and many jewelry lovers are not aware that this sparkling, vibrant gem exists. Despite this, zircon—specifically the blue variety—was added to the official list of birthstones in 1952. Though blue zircon is the most sought-after color, it comes in a range of hues, including yellow, green, red, pink, purple, orange, and brown.

Zircon has not only been in use for thousands of years, it is also the oldest gemstone on the planet, with some specimens having formed more than four billion years ago. There may even be mentions of zircon in the Bible, specifically in the Old Testament, as one of the 12 stones in Breastplate of Aaron (see Introduction). In this instance, it is referred to as jacinth or hyacinth, a name once used for the yellow, orange, red, and pink varieties of zircon. This adds an extra layer of confusion to the history of the stone, as hyacinth was also the name the Ancient Greeks gave to blue sapphire. It is likely that the earliest use of zircon in jewelry and adornment can be traced back to Ancient Persia, which is also where the stone may have gotten its name. Some scholars believe that the word "zircon" derives from to the Persian word *zargun*,

A zircon crystal

meaning gold-hued. This also suggests that the earliest known forms of zircon were the warmer colors. It is not unreasonable to assume that blue zircon would have been mistaken for sapphire by ancient cultures.

USES AND SYMBOLISM

There are examples of carved red and brown zircon intaglio from Ancient Greece, going back to the 3rd century BCE, and the brown, red, and golden varieties of the stone were highly prized in Ancient Rome. Although we know the stone was used and beloved by these cultures, it is impossible to separate its mythology from that of the other "hyacinth," blue sapphire. It does seem that the stone was believed to be able to protect travelers, and ensure them a warm welcome at at any inn or resting place along the way.

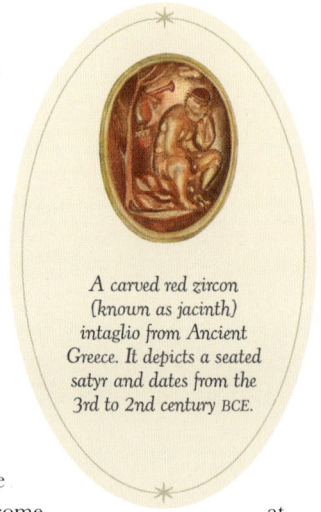

A carved red zircon (known as jacinth) intaglio from Ancient Greece. It depicts a seated satyr and dates from the 3rd to 2nd century BCE.

Skipping forward through history, we have documentation of how medieval-era Europeans felt about the stone, believing it to ward off evil spirits, bring on restful sleep, promote wisdom, and enhance the wearer's intellect. It was also thought to protect against the plague. The stone seems to have had particular importance in the Middle East during this time, with the encyclopedist and physician Ibn al-Akfani devoting a very large portion of his 14th-century treatise on gemstones, *Kitāb nuhab al-dahā'ir fī ahwāl al-jawāhir* (*The selection of treasures regarding precious stones*) being devoted to the many varieties of jacinth, or zircon. Today, zircon is regarded by many as a stone that promotes emotional balance, motivation, and in the case of the yellow and gold varieties, prosperity.

Blue zircon experienced particular popularity as a stone used in mourning jewelry during the Victorian era, and this vogue for brilliant-blue zircon meant that larger specimens in this shade were all but gone by the middle of the 20th century. Prior to World War II, it was not uncommon to find gem dealers selling blue zircon in sizes up to 25 carats, yet finding a stone of even 10 carats is fairly rare today. Much like the similarly misunderstood spinel, it is difficult to imagine a stone with this much demand becoming all but unknown in today's world, though there is a growing interest in the rainbow of sparkling colors that zircon can provide.

SOURCES AND PHYSICAL PROPERTIES

Though zircon is quite hard, at 7.5 on the Mohs scale, it is also brittle, and prone to chipping at its edges. Despite the need to take extra care when wearing and storing zircon, the stone is prized for its incredible fire and luster, rivaling that of diamond and spinel. Historically mined in Sri Lanka, one of the world's oldest and most plentiful sources of beautiful gems, the mineral has since been found in many other locations around the world, with Australia now accounting for the largest share of the world's zircon production. It is also mined in Cambodia, Madagascar, Canada, Tanzania, and Myanmar. Much like any other colored stone, the value of zircon is determined by its depth of color, clarity, and size, with blue, green, and red stones being the most valuable. Stones can be, and often are, heat-treated to create the desirable vibrant blue color, but untreated, natural stones will fetch a premium price among jewelry and gem collectors.

ZIRCON

NOTABLE JEWELS

One of the most ardent collectors of zircon jewelry was an unlikely character, the heiress to a cereal fortune with exceptional taste in fine gems, Marjorie Merriweather Post. She not only purchased many historical jewelry treasures, such as tiaras and necklaces made for Napoleon Bonaparte's second wife, Empress Marie-Louise, and diamonds that once belonged to Marie Antoinette, but she amassed a collection of important 20th century jewels, as well. She began donating pieces of her jewelry collection to the Smithsonian National Museum of Natural History in the 1960s, and urged many of her wealthy socialite friends to do the same, helping to grow the museum's noteworthy and spectacular collection of gemstones. Among her treasured jewels were many pieces set with striking blue zircon, including a beautiful necklace made by Cartier, set with 21 graduated, round, sky-blue zircons, surrounded by sparkling diamonds. Also within her capacious jewelry boxes were a matched, neon-blue zircon and spinel Art Deco bracelet and dress clip, both fashioned by the incredible jeweler Joel Helft in the 1930s.

Aside from housing some of these spectacular jewels, the Smithsonian also holds the world's largest zircon gems, with the record holder being a 118-carat, brown zircon from Sri Lanka. This may not seem very large when compared to some of the outstanding examples of big gems, such as the gigantic El Dorado Topaz, but zircon crystals are usually quite small, making an 118-carat stone a very large specimen, indeed. Though most of the larger zircon specimens are brown or reddish-brown, the second-largest stone is a blue zircon from Thailand, weighing 103 carats. The museum also boasts an incredibly unusual green specimen from Sri Lanka, weighing 97 carats.

An earring and necklace set comprised of bright-blue zircon and diamonds, made by Cartier in 1939, and owned by Marjorie Merriweather Post.

An Art Deco dress clip set with bright-blue zircon and diamonds, made by Cartier circa 1930, and owned by Marjorie Merriweather Post.

Tanzanite

The last of our stones for December, and for the year, could be considered a very modern stone, having only been discovered in 1967 and added to the list of birthstones in 2002.

Tanzanite, with its alluring shades of deep blue, hails from the Merelani hills of Tanzania, as the name suggests. Initially thought to be a variety of olivine, then a variety of sapphire, it is, instead, part of the zoisite family of stones. Though zoisite comes in other colors, tanzanite is both the most famous, and most sought-after variety. One of the unusual factors determining the relatively high price of tanzanite is the incredibly small mining area it can be found in, entirely within the Simanjiro district of Tanzania. It is one of the only gemstones in the world that is found exclusively in one location.

THE BASICS

+ **Tanzanite:** *A variety of zoisite*

+ **Colors:** *Purple, blue, brown, yellow, green*

+ **Hardness:** *6–6.5*

+ **Sourced:** *Tanzania*

Tanzanite is also notable for its incredibly strong pleochroism, meaning that it shows different colors when viewed at different angles. Other gems also display this phenomenon, but the effect is especially distinct, and striking, in tanzanite, alternately appearing blue, violet, and dark red. Some examples of tanzanite also show the phenomenon known as color change, with blues appearing darker under fluorescent light, and violet showing more strongly in incandescent light. This magical-seeming gem was, unfortunately, unknown until the 20th century, which means that there is no older history or record of the stone, but it has certainly fascinated jewelry lovers in the modern world. Some regard it as a stone with the ability to promote peace, facilitate communication, and enhance focus.

A tanzanite crystal

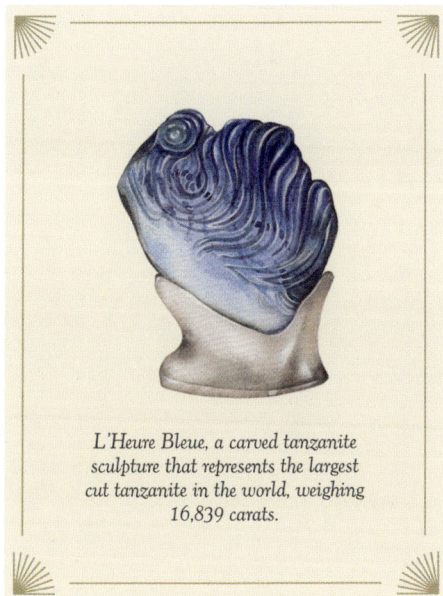

L'Heure Bleue, a carved tanzanite sculpture that represents the largest cut tanzanite in the world, weighing 16,839 carats.

Though there is only a short history of mining this beautiful gem, discoveries of gigantic tanzanite crystals have been made. The largest rough crystal was discovered in 2020 and weighs 25,515 carats. This is much larger than the previous record holder, a stone known as Mawenzi, found in 2005 and weighing 16,839 carats. The largest cut tanzanite, known as L'Heure Bleue, is a deep, indigo blue abstract sculpture resembling an undulating wave, or perhaps a flame, weighing 703 carats after carving.

The unique locality of tanzanite has afforded the Tanzanian government an opportunity to enrich its local economy by awarding mining rights not only to large groups, but small miners, as well. This decision, along with a 2010 law prohibiting the export of tanzanite rough larger than one gram, has created an industry that allows the people of Tanzania to benefit from the geological riches that have been discovered within their country, and has created new jobs in the form of gem miners and cutters alike.

TANZANITE

IMPOSTER GEMS

The science of gemology is relatively new compared to the history of humans using gemstones for adornment. Though there has been an avid interest in identifying and evaluating gemstones since the time of Ancient Greece, the tools and equipment necessary for truly studying gems in a scientific manner have only existed for a few centuries. While many texts and treatises on stones have been written in the last 2,000 years, tools such as microscopes did not exist until the late 16th century, and the practice of identifying gems and minerals by their chemical composition, instead of their crystal structure, was not discovered until the early 19th century. Because of these relatively new methods of identifying gems, many colored gemstones were not known to be their own distinct types of minerals until pretty recently. Some of these stones were misidentified, usually as more valuable and rare gems, such as spinel being mistaken for ruby, or tourmaline being mistaken for emerald.

In the case of red spinel and tourmaline being mistaken for ruby, it is entirely likely that such stones were known to be something distinct from true corundum rubies, and that "ruby" was simply used to refer to all manner of dark-pink and red precious gems. One clue that hints at the knowledge of these stones being something different is the use of the name "balas ruby" to refer to pink and red spinel, well before any scientific distinction between rubies and spinels was possible. Some of these examples of "false" rubies are quite famous, with a few of them still being called by their incorrect names.

One such stone is the famed Black Prince's Ruby, a large 170-carat, red stone set into the British Imperial State Crown. As the name suggests, this irregular cabochon-cut stone was thought to be a ruby from the 14th century onward, though it seems that there was some knowledge of it being different from a corundum ruby by the 16th century. King Henry VIII's 1521 inventory of the royal jewels lists it as a "great balas ruby," a name given to red spinel, which indeed, it is. Despite this distinction in naming, it was not until 1783 that spinel was determined to be a chemically distinct mineral, not part of the corundum family that ruby belongs to.

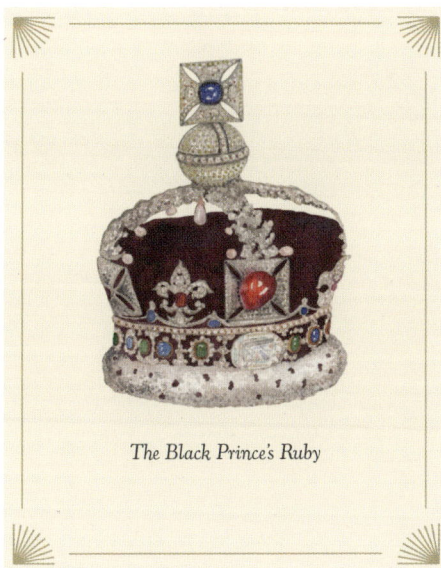

The Black Prince's Ruby

IMPOSTER GEMS

Another notable ruby imposter is the Menshikov Ruby, yet another significant red spinel set into a royal crown. Perched atop the Imperial Crown of Russia, this stone was purchased in China in 1702. The large red orb was set into the crown when it was made for Catherine the Great in 1762. Weighing just over 398 carats, this stone is believed to be the second-largest spinel in the world. The stone was referred to in contemporary texts as a "lal" stone, a word used to refer to red and pink spinels and tourmalines in Russia, so it is likely that it was known to be something different from a true corundum ruby, yet the name Menshikov Ruby has stuck.

Two of the more whimsical ruby imposters are cut into fanciful shapes, and are also part of royal collections. The first, Caesar's Ruby, has changed hands multiple times, eventually ending up as property of the Russian monarchy, and residing at the Kremlin in Moscow, today. It is a bright, deep-fuchsia stone in the shape of a bunch of grapes, with a history going back to the late 15th century, when it was in the possession of King Charles IX of France. For centuries, it was thought to be the world's largest ruby at 260 carats, and it caused considerable consternation when it was eventually discovered, in 1925, that this lovely gemmy fruit was, in fact, a rubellite tourmaline. The other stone, known as the Côte de Bretagne spinel, is a 105-carat, pinkish-orange spinel cut into the form of what is described as a "fat oriental dragon." This stone, looking like nothing so much as a delicious gummy candy, was once part of an elaborate Insignia of the Order of the Golden Fleece, a badge of honor denoting membership in the Catholic order of chivalry after which it is named. This insignia, made as a pendant to be hung from a ribbon, also featured one of history's most fascinating and mysterious gems, the French Blue diamond. Both the spinel dragon and the French Blue went missing when the French crown jewels were stolen, during the height of the French Revolution, in 1792. The spinel dragon was miraculously recovered, while the French Blue was recut and presumed missing for nearly two centuries, when it was proven that the infamous Hope Diamond was, in fact, what was left of the missing stone.

Menshikov Ruby

Caesar's Ruby

Côte de Bretagne spinel

IMPOSTER GEMS

THE FOUR 'C'S

---- ✱ ----

In the ancient world, gemstones were rare, and acquired through laborious means without the benefit of modern technology. This meant that gemstones were highly prized, even if they were not necessarily "perfect." In our globalized modern world, with massive mining efforts and major advances in technology, we have access to just about every gem and precious metal imaginable. This, of course, means that there is a wide range of material available on the market, and it is not all equal. There has to be some sort of system for determining the value of gems, so that they can be priced accordingly.

Most gemstones are graded using a set of characteristics referred to as the four 'C's: cut, color, clarity, and carat weight. Of course, not every birthstone on this list can be measured using all four of these characteristics (pearl and turquoise, for instance, would not be judged based on their clarity), but it remains a good general means of assessing the value of both colored gemstones, and diamonds.

Cut

A quality gemstone of high value should be cut in a way that enhances the color, achieves maximum brilliance, and loses no light through the back. This is the characteristic that humans have the most control over, though clarity and color can be altered somewhat by using heat and irradiation. The final polish of the gem is also considered as part of the quality of its cut.

Color

Color is the most critical factor in determining the value of any gem, at any size. All colored gemstones are judged based on the tone and intensity of their color (tone is the depth of color, from light to dark, while intensity is the strength of color). Different gems have different ranges of tone and intensity that are considered most valuable. For instance, high-quality emeralds are expected to be green, with a tone in the medium-to-dark range, with medium intensity. Too much intensity, or strength of color, and the stone looks muddy and dark.

Clarity

Clarity refers to how many visible inclusions are in the stone. Opaque gems such as pearl, turquoise, and sardonyx are not measured by their clarity, and some stones, such as emeralds, are given more leeway for visible inclusions than other gems. Though stones without inclusions are more valuable, inclusions themselves can actually help gemologists determine where a stone was originally mined.

Carat Weight

Carat weight is the total weight of a cut stone. Carats are the unit of measurement used when weighing gemstones, where 1 carat is equal to 200mg. The word "carat" is derived from "carob," because the seeds of the carob tree are very uniform in size and weight, and made for a handy unit of measurement in the ancient world. Though the carat weight of a gemstone does factor into its value, a stone of exceptional color and clarity, but lower carat weight, will be worth more than a large stone of less desirable color, with more visible inclusions.

STONE CUTS

Cabochon Cut

(also known as "en cabochon")
One of the oldest known stone
cuts. The bottom of the stone is
wide and flat; the top is shaped
into a rounded dome.

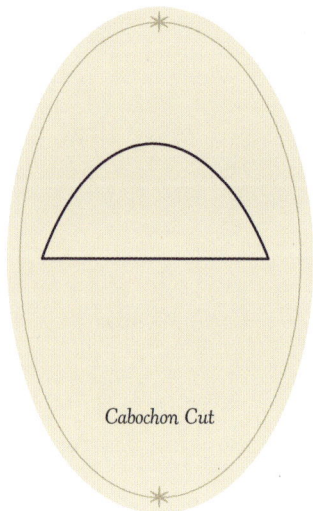

Cabochon Cut

Rose Cut

A traditional cut, where the
bottom is wide, flat, and
unfaceted, and the top is
domed and covered with
triangular facets.

Rose Cut

Step Cut

A cut often used in rectangular
and square gemstones, with
large facets arranged in rows,
that run parallel to the stone's
widest part.

Brilliant Cut

Often seen in diamonds, with
a modern version created in
the 1950s, this consists of facets
radiating out from the crown (top)
to the girdle (edge) of the stone.

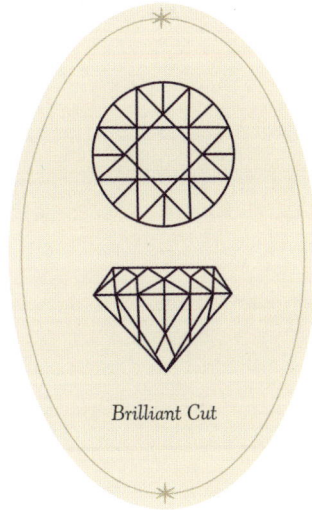

Step Cut

Brilliant Cut

GLOSSARY

— ✳ —

ASTERISM A phenomenon seen in some gemstones in which very fine, needlelike inclusions create the illusion of a star on the surface of the stone when viewed under a single light source.

CABOCHON A cut of gemstone that involves shaping and polishing, usually with a flat bottom and domed surface, as opposed to cutting facets.

CAMEO A stone with a design or portrait carved in relief (the opposite of an intaglio).

CARAT A unit of weight used for measuring gemstones. The weight of a carat has changed over time, but it is now equivalent to 200mg.

CARDINAL STONES A group of gems considered to be more precious than all others. Currently, cardinal stones include diamonds, emeralds, sapphires, and rubies. Prior to the discovery of large amethyst deposits in Brazil in the 1870s, amethysts were also considered precious and rare enough to be called cardinal stones.

CLOISONNÉ A type of decorative metalwork, in which colored enamel, glass, or cut gemstones are separated by means of flat strips of wire. This technique can be traced back to Ancient Egypt.

FACET A flat, polished surface cut or ground into a gemstone. The arrangement, and number, of facets on a stone are determined by the desired final shape and cut style.

FIRE A term used to describe the sparkle and flashes of color that occur when light hits a gemstone, also known as dispersion.

GEODE A cavity within a rock that is lined with crystals. Very large geodes, such as the amethyst geodes found in Brazil and Uruguay, are informally known as "crystal caves."

INTAGLIO A stone with a design or portrait engraved into it (the opposite of a cameo).

IRRADIATION A method of treating gemstones with artificial radiation, in order to enhance the color, clarity, or both. The most commonly irradiated gemstones are vibrant-blue varieties of topaz, which do not occur naturally, and usually start out as brown or colorless topaz before treatment.

JAINISM A religion originating in India, in the 6th century BCE, which teaches that enlightenment can be achieved through nonviolence, and reducing harm to all living things. It centers on the belief of an eternal soul, and reincarnation, though there is no worship of a central god or deity.

MATRIX This term can refer to the rock material that gemstones are embedded in before extraction, but also any penetrating inclusions within the stone. Turquoise often shows evidence of matrix, seen as dark lines and stripes within the cut stone.

MEXICA PEOPLE An Indigenous people of central Mexico, commonly referred to as Aztec. Mexica is the name they would have used to refer to themselves.

PALLADIUM A silvery-white metal resembling platinum. It is fairly rare and has only been in use in jewelry since 1939.

PARURE A term used to describe a set of jewels intended to be worn together, often consisting of a matching necklace, earrings, bracelet(s), and pin(s), but can also include tiaras, belts, and less common forms of jewelry such as armlets or decorative buttons. A smaller set, composed of two matching pieces, such as a necklace and earrings, is called a demi-parure.

PLEOCHROISM An optical phenomenon that causes a stone to appear two, or more, different colors when viewed at different angles. The effect is not the same as "color change," a phenomenon that causes stones such as alexandrite to appear different colors under different types of light.

SAUTOIR A French term that describes a long necklace that holds a tassel or other pendant. A sautoir is often much longer than a standard necklace, sometimes reaching the waist.

ABOUT THE AUTHOR

--- ✱ ---

Melise Ozkardesler

Melise is a goldsmith trained in ancient techniques, a history enthusiast, and an antique jewelry collector. She is also the creator and host of the Ancient History Jewelry Stories video and podcast series, which has garnered a following of thousands of fans. Combining a passion for antique jewelry, ancient history, and the beauty of the natural world, with technical insight as a goldsmith, Melise tells stories highlighting how our age-old love of adornment has created what is perhaps the most meaningful way to engage with our shared history, approaching jewelry as the most personal form of art. Melise's love of history, along with her Turkish heritage, has fostered a lifelong curiosity about the ancient world, and the cultures that preceded us.

Born in Cologne, Germany, a colorful and free-spirited childhood saw Melise living in exciting places such as Miami Beach, New York, Costa Rica, and Barcelona, presenting a unique opportunity to experience the world and learn several languages. She now lives in Brooklyn with her husband, tuxedo cat, and sizable vintage clothing collection. When she is not at her bench crafting new jewelry, she can be found at the nearest farmer's market, thrift store, antique shop, or museum.

INDEX

143

A VERBENA BOOK
© David and Charles, Ltd 2025

Verbena is an imprint of David and Charles, Ltd
Suite A, Tourism House, Pynes Hill, Exeter,
EX2 5WS

Text © Melise Ozkardesler 2025
Layout © David and Charles, Ltd 2025

First published in the UK and USA in 2025

A catalogue record for this book is available from
the British Library.

ISBN-13: 9781446315644 hardback
ISBN-13: 9781446315651 EPUB

This book has been printed on paper from
approved suppliers and made from pulp from
sustainable sources.

MIX
Paper | Supporting
responsible forestry
FSC
www.fsc.org FSC® C136333

Printed in China through Asia Pacific Offset for:
David and Charles, Ltd
Suite A, Tourism House, Pynes Hill, Exeter,
EX2 5WS

10 9 8 7 6 5 4 3 2 1

Publishing Director: Ame Verso
Senior Commissioning Editor: Lizzie Kaye
Publishing Manager: Jeni Chown
Editor: Jessica Cropper
Copy Editor: Anna Southgate
Lead Designer: Sam Staddon
Designer: Marieclare Mayne
Pre-press Designer: Susan Reansbury
Illustrations: Alena Solonshchikova
Production Manager: Beverley Richardson

David and Charles publishes high-quality books on
a wide range of subjects. For more information visit
www.davidandcharles.com.

Follow us on Instagram by searching for
@verbena_books and @dandcbooks.

Layout of the digital edition of this book may vary
depending on reader hardware and display settings.